My BEST TO YOU FOREVER

DEVOTIONALS FOR YOUR PRIVATE MOMENTS WITH GOD

Donald C. Hancock

ISBN-10:153746583X

ISBN-13:978-1537465838

The following books and others may be found at:

www.amazonbooks.com

A Message For All Time (A Novel)

The Message Takes Wings (A Novel)

The Message Lives On (A Novel)

The Quest

The White Cliffs Of Dover

A Lesson From History

A Penny Saved

A Penny For Your Thoughts

Pennies From Heaven

Remembering Our Buddies

The Women Who Flew In World War II

The Hero

The Universe Indeed

Next Door Neighbors

Neighbors No More

The Family At Fair Haven

Life After Fair Haven

DEDICATION

I dedicate this book to God, for whom I write, to my family and friends, for whom I publish, and to my Dear Wife, who has always been the 'wind beneath my wings'. I also dedicate it to all who have encouraged my writing by reading my books over the years

MY BEST TO YOU FOREVER

CONTENTS

INTRODUCTION

Several years ago I retired as a Chaplain in a State School for the Developmentally Disabled, where I had ministered full time for 21 years. Before that I had been a Pastor for 14 years. So, after retirement I was delighted to be asked, about twice a month, to prepare a ten minute devotional for my own Sunday School Department at First Baptist Church of Augusta, Georgia. The department is made up of Senior Adults, men and women, who accepted my offerings graciously.

Since each devotional was prepared prayerfully and with a great deal of thought and preparation, I thought that it might be helpful to other folks. So, when I had collected enough devotionals, I published them in a little book called, "My Best To You Each Morning", hoping it would be helpful for your own devotional use. The book was so well received that I prepared a second and third volume of devotionals. This is my fourth volume. I hope that it will also prove to be helpful. That is my purpose in offering all four of these books to you.

Rev. Donald C. Hancock, Augusta, Georgia.

October, 2016. donh1654@comcast.net

MY BEST TO YOU FOREVER

CHAPTER 1: GOD KNOWS OUR LIFE FROM START TO FINISH

My favorite popular band has always been the Glenn Miller Orchestra. Even in the second grade I was already enjoying his records on the radio. Of course, Glenn Miller was killed at the close of World War two and one of his saxophonists, Tex Beneke became the Director.

In 1948, I lived in Jacksonville and was a sophomore in high school and played trombone in the high school band. I also played in a small "Garage" type jazz band that played "big band" music. It was sponsored by a middle aged lady who had been a singer with a big band in her younger days. One night during practice, she put all six of us in her car and took us to the main auditorium in Jacksonville where the Glenn Miller Orchestra was giving a concert. She had made arrangements for us to go back stage and meet Tex Beneke and the band. I remember that she bragged on us by saying to Tex that he need not worry. Her band would be ready to fill in when The Glenn Miller group got too old to play, or at least something of that nature.

One of my favorite videos is the movie, "The Glenn Miller Story". Jimmy Stewart plays Glenn Miller and June Allyson plays his wife. In the movie, the band is in the middle of making the movie, "Sun Valley Serenade" in which Glenn and his Orchestra are featured throughout the movie. In "The Glenn Miller Story", Glenn's wife comes into the studio and brings Glenn a letter from the Army in which his commission as an officer has been approved. He would be a band director. This movie, "Sun Valley Serenade", would be the last time he plays as a civilian. He becomes a very successful band director in the Army and is even given permission to form his own band and play his old Glenn Miller style. As the war is closing down, he takes off from England to play for the troops in Paris, but, as his plane is crossing the English Channel on a very foggy day, the plane disappears and it is never known for sure what happened. That was a very sad movie at the end and, of course, it was very sad in real life also.

Just the other night, I saw the movie, "Sun Valley Serenade" on Television. It is the black and white movie he was making just before joining the Army. It seemed so very strange to see the real Glenn Miller playing in that movie, having a wonderful time, not realizing that in just a very short time he would be in the Army and within months after that, at a time when he had every right to be expecting a wonderful future career, he would be taken from his wife and friends.

There I was, knowing the beginning and ending of his life and knowing that, as he played that trombone with such enjoyment, he had absolutely no knowledge of what was going to happen.

For a few moments it was as though I were seeing Glenn's life as God sees our lives. God DOES know our lives from beginning to end, you know, even as we smilingly enjoy playing the tunes of our lives. One might think, "Then, if God knew that Glenn Miller was going to die in a plane crash on that foggy day, why did not God give him a little "nudge" just to wait until the fog lifted before attempting the flight? I believe the answer to that question is that, "If Glenn Miller still had things that God wanted him to finish in his earth life, that God would certainly have kept him safe and alive. But, to my way of thinking at least, Glenn had already accomplished everything that was in God's plan for him. Yes, many people were sad and felt that their lives would suffer when Glenn died, certainly his wife, his son, and his band would feel that way. But so it was also when Christ died. Christ Himself recognized that there was a possibility that he could have lived on for a while. That is why He prayed that prayer in the Garden of Gethsemane, "Father, if it be Thy will, let this cup, the cup of death, pass. But, nevertheless, not my will but thine be done." The fact that Christ DID die means, to me, that He had already accomplished EVERYTHING that God had planned for Him to do. The same was true of Glenn Miller. The same is true of you and me. I believe that God knows our lives from beginning to end right now. And not one of us will die until we have done every last thing that is in God's plan for us to do. As someone has said, "It doesn't get any better than that!"

Dear Father, help us to trust our lives and our future into your hands, knowing that nothing can take us away from your plan for our lives. In Jesus' name, Amen.

CHAPTER 2: OUR QUIET MOMENTS

Text John 1:47-49.

In the verses just before our text, Jesus was just beginning his ministry and was calling the ones that he wanted to be his Apostles – his first disciples. He had found Philip and had said, "Follow me!" Philip had done so. Then Philip quickly went to his brother, Nathanael. "We have found the Messiah and He is Jesus of Nazareth!" Nathanael must have had a bit of the carefulness of Thomas. He did come but was not completely sold by what his brother had told him. Then, our text says, " Jesus saw Nathanael coming to Him and he said, 'Behold, an Israelite indeed, in whom is no guile.' Nathanael said to Jesus, "Whence knowest thou me?" Jesus said, "Before Philip called you, when you were under the fig tree, I saw you." Nathanael answered and said unto Him, "Rabbi, You are the son of God. You are the King of Israel!"

Nathanael was not convinced by Philip. But, when Jesus mentioned Nathanael's "Quiet Moment" beneath the fig tree, it was as if they were speaking a "secret language" that only they understood. We do not know what Nathanael was doing or thinking under that fig tree. But it was as though Jesus was really saying, "Nathanael, I know what you were wishing and praying for in the deepest part of your spirit, when you were under that fig tree, and I want you to know that I am part of The Father's answer to that prayer!" Nathanael knew that Jesus could not have known the significance of his quiet moment under the fig tree unless He had supernatural powers. Thus, He must have been sent by God Himself.

I do not know when you had your last "quiet moment" or what it was about. But I am sure that God was listening and that He heard what was on your heart. It might have been something that you were worried about or something that you are afraid will happen. It might have been about a decision that you are facing and you do not know what to do. You might have been feeling guilt or anger or any number of other emotions. But whatever it was about, you can be sure that our Father "saw you under your "fig tree" and that He heard your concern.

But you might be saying, "If He heard me, why didn't he answer me? I am still afraid or I still do not know what to do about the decision that I am facing. Why hasn't He helped me?"

My answer to that is that, when God hears you, it

does not mean that He is necessarily going to do just what you are asking Him to do or that He is going to do it exactly when you want Him to do it. God knows what is best for you. He also knows when is the best time for your prayer to be answered. That is why we need to pay attention to Jesus' model prayer. Not the "Our Father" prayer but the other one – His prayer in the Garden that night before His trial. Remember that He prayed, "Oh my Father, if it be possible, let this cup pass from me, nevertheless, not my will but thine be done." In reality He was saying, "Father, this is what I would really like for You to do – let me stay here and continue teaching with my disciples for a while, but I know that You know what is best so please let what you know is best be done."

With that in mind, I would like for you to use Jesus' prayer as your guide. Like this: "Dear Father, I have this decision that is facing me and it is really keeping me worried. I don't have a clue as to what I should do. I would like very much for you to give me a clear answer as to what I should do, and please help me to know it right away. It is all that I can think about. I would really like to be able to stop worrying about it. But, Father, I know that, if what I am asking is not best for me or if You want to wait until later to help me, then I know that You have a very good reason for that decision, so please help me to accept that decision with faith that You always know what is best." If we can all begin to pray like that in every "quiet moment" that we have with God, then not only can we be sure of a good outcome, knowing that however God chooses to answer our prayers will be the best possible way for it to turn out, but we will sleep better and do a lot less worrying in the mean time.

Let me leave you with this example. You might have heard it before but it will illustrate what I am saying here. During high school I felt the call to the ministry, but I was not really sure if it really was God calling me or whether it was just what I wanted to do. So I prayed and prayed. For three years I prayed without a clear answer. Finally, after all that praying, in which I am sure that I sometimes felt terribly "let down" by God, finally, one afternoon when I was home alone, feeling very desperate, I actually got on my knees in the living room and prayed, "Please, Father, please help me to know if You are really calling me, please give me a sign." For some reason that God only knows, the time had come. The door bell rang at that very moment. A gentleman introduced himself by name and said that he was the Pastor of a Pentecostal Church two blocks away. I did not know the gentleman nor had I had any dealings with that church. The Pastor just said that he felt led of God to bring this pamphlet to someone at this house. He gave me the pamphlet and it was titled, "The Call of God". I told him about my prayer and we both felt very happy that God had just given me a rather clear and dramatic answer to my three year old prayer. The wait had certainly taxed my patience and my faith, but the outcome was worth the wait.

Prayer: Dear Father, help us to see that You are always For us and not against us, that you are always giving us what is best for us. Help us to trust you always. In Jesus' name, Amen

DONALD C. HANCOCK

CHAPTER 3: WHO KNOWS WHAT SIMPLE THING MIGHT BLESS SOMEONE?

When I was in high school I had a close friend named John Howell. We were both in the band. He played trumpet and I played trombone. He was the son of a local Baptist Minister. We were both feeling the call to the ministry, but, since he had grown up in the church, he had had more experience than I had. So, on several occasions we had some long talks and he gave me some very helpful counseling about God and His ways.

John was just an average student in high school, but when he and I got to Stetson University, it was as though his motivation went sky high. He only got one grade in four years under an A. That is because "Madam" Thornton, the German Professor did not believe in giving A's. Thus she gave John her highest grade, a B. John had, as a goal, to make a letter in Sports. He was too light for football and too short for basketball, but he got a Letter as Manager of the Baseball Team. He was outstanding in Drama and in College Leadership. He was voted to be an "Out Standing Senior" and had many, many honors at Stetson. He preached at a small church while in Stetson, the Caccia Baptist Church. He asked me to "fill in" for him several Sundays, thus giving me my very first experience in preaching at a church. When he went to Seminary, he did not go to an ordinary Seminary like I did. He went to a Seminary in Scotland, and they were glad to get him. He came back and became the Pastor of the First Baptist Church of Deland, Florida – our College Church. At some point, he married Bettye Jean Henderson, his college sweet heart. B.J (as she was called) was also an outstanding student at Stetson who won many honors while there.

Later, he became the pastor of Crescent Hill Baptist of Louisville, Kentucky. It was a large and very outstanding Baptist church, one attended by many of the Professors of the Southern Baptist Seminary in Louisville. John's flame burned very brightly and yet very briefly. He died quite young, I believe, with a brain tumor.

Yes, John was quite an influence on me, both in high school and in college. Our talks together, his allowing me to get valuable preaching experience, and his remarkable record at Stetson and in the ministry, were all a blessing to my later ministry. But you would never guess in a lifetime what I consider his greatest contribution to my life. It happened one night at a school friend's party. I heard an instrument playing and there was John sitting in a chair in the living room and a dozen friends were sitting on the floor around him. They were all singing the sort of songs we sang in those days and John was playing anything they wanted to sing. There was "I've Been Working On the Railroad" and "Cum Ba Ya" and many more. John was playing his Ukulele and he didn't have to have music or anything. He could immediately play anything they wanted to sing. If he knew the tune he could play it. It was the neatest thing I had ever heard. I wanted to do that too! I started saving for a Uke immediately.

I did get a ukulele and got a book to go with it. I learned a bunch of the chords. I could never have learned all of them, but I learned enough to play several songs. The first song I learned was "Ain't She Sweet?". I still know those chords 'til this day.

I didn't learn to play like John did, not then, anyway. But I wanted to. It remained until I became a pastor, many years later that I began to play the uke again in order to work with the young people. Then, when I became a Chaplain I began to use a ukulele every day as I went to the different cottages and sang with the residents. Playing the ukulele, just like John, became one of my every day activities. So, 20 years after John inadvertently influenced me to play the ukulele, I was able to do exactly what I had admired John doing at the party that night. I did it for 21 years until I retired. I still do it once a month when I go to have a sing along with the residents at Brookdale Assisted Living. We do it in our Sunday School Department sometimes too. There is simply no way to put a value tag on that blessing that my friend John gave me.

John never knew how much his influence would bless my life. That is true with you, too. You might never know just how much "simply being yourself" might bless someone's life, maybe, like John, without you ever knowing it. But that's OK too. It might be something that they learn from you, like knitting or crocheting or how to fix some minor plumbing problem. It might be a favorite thing that you say, like, "If it's God's will it will work!". It might be as simple as your smile or your hug or the way that you laugh. It might be as complicated as how you decide if something is right or wrong. It could be bringing her soup when she is sick or a dozen eggs that your chickens laid. It could just be your faithfulness to Sunday School and Church. Someone might say, on a rainy Sunday morning, "I would sure love to stay in bed but I know Mary will be there so I guess I had better get up and start moving."

John was simply being himself that night when he

ed his ukulele at that party. But he blessed my life for 66 years.

So, please take this suggestion seriously. God has built some things into your life that will bless certain people that you will meet. You do not know which things these are or who will be the folks that these things will bless. You do not need to know. Just believe me that it is true. You do not know if the blessing will be just once or if it will still be operating years from now. Just 2 Sundays ago we sang a song in here, "All That Thrills My Soul Is Jesus". There was a man in our Church Association who liked to sing that at Association meetings. It was just a little high for him and he had to strain to get it but in his straining he was blessing me for the next 59 years and he never knew it.

The best thing that we can all do is ask God to use us each day, just as we are, just as He has made us, or just as He might want to change us.

Prayer: Dear Father. Help us to trust in the unique personality that you have given us and help us to dedicate our words and our actions and even the nuances of who we are to the purpose of doing Your will and being a blessing to those about us. In Jesus' name, Amen

DONALD C. HANCOCK

CHAPTER 4: PRAY FOR OUR WORLD

I am not usually a pessimist, but when I look at our world today and especially at the humanity that lives on our planet, I must admit that I am worried. I am not worried so much about the "near future" but about what might happen when our "children's children" are grown. I can't help but believe something that I heard Pete Seeger, the folk singer, say recently when he was speaking to the New York Press Club. As I remember, it was something like this: "Humanity might not have several hundred years left if we continue as we are now. We certainly do not have another 2000 years to learn the "Golden Rule". (It has been over 2000 years since Jesus gave it to us).

I usually try to write "feel good novels" and "feel good short stories", and "feel good devotionals" but I am afraid this is not going to be one of them.

So what is it about the world that bothers me? That might sound like a silly question, since there is so much that any of us can name. It would be so easy to just lump it all together and just call it "sin". But that which we call "sin" has been with us for a long time and the world seems to have survived pretty well, if we don't count the species that haven't survived, like the dinosaurs and quite a few others. But I am worried about the survival of humanity itself.

Many worried about our survival when the atomic bomb became a threat, because, for the first time in history, mankind had at his disposal the ability to commit mass murder or suicide in one disastrous war. But now we have, added to that threat, the converging of several other threads of reality that contribute to each other.

The world is on a "slippery slope" of world wide terrorism, lack of compassion, street violence, and lack of statesmanship in government. Added to this is a new feature that has the ability to make all of these negatives much worse than they are at present. I am talking about modern technology.

Technology, especially electronics, includes computers, "very smart telephones", drone airplanes and helicopters, self driving cars, and other things that are probably on the drawing boards. As I understand it, a technician can sit at a console in some city in America and blow up an automobile in Iraq.

Technology is not "bad" in itself. It is simply a servant that greatly amplifies whatever it is serving. Whether it is serving good or evil, kindness or hate, aid in a disaster or terrorism, the American Red Cross or Isis, it makes whatever it serves faster, more efficient, and stronger. So, as technology converges with the many evils that have been around ever since God created mankind, the threat to the survival of mankind deepens. Bombs, bullets, and hate can become better able to do their job of killing, demoralizing, and shortening the life of both mankind and the planet earth.

The good news is that, as I said, technology can also serve God and His plans for mankind's future. Technology can also enhance and spread love, compassion, random kindness, positive acts of statesmanship in government, acts of self giving – all of these positive elements can "go viral", that is, be seen by millions of people on the computer and television, within the time it takes me to write this devotional. Someone fulfilling the Golden Rule in some simple or extraordinary fashion might be viewed by people all over the world. That can go a long way toward changing the world in a good way.

Someone told the story of three men who survived the sinking of a ship. The three men found a small rubber dinghy drifting and climbed aboard. It had two paddles. One of the men had a broken arm and so he could not help. The other two men began to row. They knew that the shore was about ten miles away, so they could survive if they rowed steadily in that direction. After about an hour of rowing the two men got in an argument about something that had happened the day before. One of the rowers pulled out a gun and shot the other one. "Why on earth did you do that?" shouted the third man. "Now you have to row all by yourself!"

"Well, I hate him after what he said to me two days ago!" said the shooter.

As unreasonable as the man's action seems, it is no more unreasonable than what is going on in the world today. Our earth is really like a little boat out on the vast ocean of space. We really can not afford "not to get along" with our fellow passengers.

The good news is, as I have said, today's technology can be used by God to bless all of mankind in amazing ways if we are willing to play our part. Mother Teresa was one person, just one, but look what she accomplished by putting herself in the hands of God. Your telephone, your computer, your hands, your feet, your spirit can become God's technology to move your little section of earth's little boat AWAY from future disaster instead of TOWARD it.

The ultimate GOOD NEWS is that, no matter what happens on this earth, now or in the future, God is still in charge, ultimately!

CHAPTER 5: ABOUT FAITH

I saw a statement recently that I really liked. It went something like this: "Faith is not just about making everything come out OK. Faith is also about being OK with the way everything comes out." Did you get that? Let me say it again. "Faith is not just about making everything come out OK. Faith is also about being OK with the way everything comes out."

There is much in the Bible about how faith can change things in your life. For instance, Jesus said that if you have faith as small as a grain of mustard seed, you can remove mountains. On many occasions Jesus healed people of sickness and did other miracles and said, "your faith has made you whole. These were examples of how faith can make everything come out OK.

But you and I know that faith does not ALWAYS make the changes in your life that you would like. There are mountains of things that we have sometimes prayed about to be changed and have been disappointed because change DID NOT come about. There are times when we have prayed in faith for healing in ourselves or in a loved one when healing did not come.

So, if "Faith is not just about making everything come out OK, then what IS faith about? The story of Job answers that question. Job WAS a man of faith. But everything certainly did not come out OK for him! He lost everything – his possessions, his live stock, his children, his health – all by "acts of God". He even lost that most precious of human relations, his relationship with his wife, when she said, "Oh Job, why don't you just curse God and die! Just 'get over it'!

But what did Job say? In effect he said, "Faith is not just about making everything come out OK. Faith is also about being OK with the way everything comes out." His actual statement was something like, "Even if God takes the next step and takes my life also, I will still die TRUSTING Him!"

Jesus had a similar experience in the Garden of Gethsemane. He prayed, "Father, if it is possible, let this cup (of death) pass from me. But, nevertheless, not MY will but THY WILL be done. He was saying, in effect, even though, if I could have my way, I would like to stay a while longer to be with my family and my disciples and continue teaching, I know that Your will is always the best way.

So, how does this play out for you and me? I believe that most of the unhappiness that people experience in life comes from not being OK with things in their life, certain "mountains" that they would like to see moved. This was probably more true when we were younger than it is now. We might have prayed, "God, please help me find a better job, I hate this job, please change this or that about my spouse or my children, please heal my sickness, my aching joints, my hearing loss, my poor eyesight, please change my awful neighbor." Then it might have come to, "God, please heal my loved one, please change this awful diagnosis or prognosis."

But to our chagrin, the mountains were not moved. At that point we need to realize that "Faith is also about being OK with the way that everything comes out." We need to remember that God did not give us the gift of faith just so that we could "move mountains" but also so that we could depend on Him and trust Him.

We need to realize just as Job did and just as Christ did, that 'even if everything does not turn out just as we would like for it to, our Father's plan is far better than our plan could ever be. Even if and when I die in the process, which I certainly will, I will die TRUSTING Him.

Prayer: Dear Father, please help us to finally

learn, if we do not know already, that whatever You have planned for us is better than the very best thing that we can imagine. In Jesus name. Amen.

CHAPTER 6: ALMOST A BLESSING

There is a new television commercial that I think is very suggestive of a spiritual truth. This is a commercial that the "Georgia Lottery" has been running. I hope that it will not offend you that a lottery commercial reminds me of a spiritual truth but that is the way my mind works.

Well, anyway, in this commercial a lady goes into a convenience store and starts to buy a lottery ticket. Immediately you see an armored truck pull up and several uniformed men get out and begin bringing in boxes of money that this woman is about to win with the numbers that she has in mind. She is about to become a millionaire. Then, all of a sudden, the woman says "wait".....all action stops with the men who are bringing in the money. The woman continues..."I think I will have a corndog instead". All of the action is reversed and the men take all of the millions of dollars back to the truck. You probably say to yourself, "Wow, if that lady just knew how close she came to being a millionaire!"

I really believe that that is a perfect picture of how many of the blessings come into our lives....or else, almost come into our lives but do not quite make it. For instance, I met my wife, Finetta, for the first time in November almost 60 years ago. But it was only because I visited a particular church one Sunday morning in which a visiting married couple sang a duet during the service. I went down to talk to them after the service because they had gone to a particular college where some of my friends attended. The couple invited me to their church that night and I went. When I sat down in the church, the girl that I sat down next to "happened" to be Finetta. The rest of the 60 years is history. But if I had not followed God's nudges to go to THAT church that morning and to TALK to the couple after the service and to FOLLOW their invitation to another church AND to SIT in that particular pew, I would have missed ALL of the blessings of those 60 years. As in the commercial, the possibility of those 60 years of blessings was building up all day on that Sunday as Finetta was also making her decision whether or not to be at church that night and in that particular pew or not, etc. But if I had not followed God's nudges, NONE of that would have happened.

The same is true of 18 years of living happily in our present neighborhood. The lady who lives across the street from us had a nudge from God 18 years ago to TELL us about a vacant house across the street from her. If she had decided NOT to follow that nudge, we would have missed those 18 years of blessing.

Are you sensitive to God's nudges? If you have a "feeling" that "it would be a good thing to DO this or SAY that", do you follow that nudge or do you let the part of your personality that considers convenience or shyness or extra trouble "talk you out of it". For instance, "Oh, she probably wouldn't want to hear that" or "If I stop to tell him about that it will take too much time" or "If I call her just to say we missed her at Sunday School she will think I am being silly!"

Let me suggest this. If you get an urge to do something where someone else is involved, just ask yourself, "Is this a GOOD thing? Is it something that promises to be helpful? Is there any way, as far as I can see, that it might HURT someone?" If the answers to these questions are to your liking, then just say, quickly, "Is this what You want, God?" If you still think it is a Good thing, then go ahead and do it, without considering whether it is going to be hard for you to do or convenient or embarrassing or whatever.

Chances are that, if what you thought of doing passes all of these tests, it is a "nudge" from God. Chances are also good that there will be blessings coming out of that action – blessings to you or to someone else or maybe to both.

CHAPTER 7: BE MY TENNIS BALL

I go to Brookdale Assisted Living once a month for a sing along. This past Monday when I was there, one of the ladies had a walker with two new tennis balls on its two back legs. I think you have all seen tennis balls on walkers. I decided to use the tennis balls as a teaching tool. I said, "I believe Mary has new tennis balls on her walker. I wonder why they put those tennis balls on there."

One lady said, "To keep it from slipping when it is supposed to be standing still." I said, "That makes sense."

Another lady said, "That tennis ball also helps the walker to glide alone smoothly when you want to move forward."

A gentleman added, "It acts as a shock absorber when you pick the walker up and put it down. The tennis ball lets it down more gently."

I said, "You know, it occurred to me that each of us can be like a tennis ball to each other!"

"How is that?" asked one of the other ladies.

"Well, the first thing that you mentioned is that it helps you to keep from slipping when you are supposed to be standing still. When you are using a walker it is usually when your legs have been hurt or you are weaker than usual because of sickness or age. So, you are already vulnerable. You are depending on the walker to give you stability. If it should suddenly slip a little bit, it can make you loose balance and fall. That is where the tennis ball comes in so handy. It keeps the walker from slipping. And that is exactly how we can be like a tennis ball to each other.

There are times when we are more vulnerable than usual, like when we are feeling bad, or we didn't get a good night's sleep, or we just got some bad news from the family or from the doctor. At times like that that we can be like a tennis ball to each other. When we see a friend showing signs that he or she is under stress – they have been crying or their face is red with anger, or they act a little confused, that's when we can be of help. We can be considerate of their feelings, speak gently and softly, maybe ask what is wrong and if you can be of help. If they do not want to talk, respect their privacy but if they confide, do what you can to help them feel better.

I recently had a minor "fender bender". No one was hurt but I was a bit upset and was not sure what I should do. A complete stranger assured me that everything was going to be all right and another stranger offered to use his phone to find the number of my insurance company and let me talk with them. Another stranger called the police. All of that was very helpful to me in my "shaken up" state of mind. They were acting like "tennis balls" for me and I was very grateful. You and I can do that same thing for each other here at Brookdale. Do you agree?" They did.

The second use of the tennis balls that you mentioned was to help the walker glide smoothly when we are trying to move forward. Again, we can be helpful to each other when we are trying to move ahead instead of slipping backward or just sitting still. There are a number of things that "age" tends to do to us. We slow up physically. We might slow up mentally. We might even seem to be loosing ground or slipping backward. That is when we can be like tennis balls to each other. We can encourage each other. We can invite each other to "do things with us" in order to stay active. We can spend some time thinking of ways to help each other think positively about living every day that God gives us for the rest of our lives.

Lastly, as the tennis ball cushions the impact of the walker when it hits the floor, we can help "cushion" the impact of whatever difficulties that each of us face in our everyday lives. We can act as cushions by loving, helping, and just "being there" for each other. So, let's all be like the tennis balls on the walker, to each other, every day.

CHAPTER 8: A NEAR DEATH EXPERIENCE

My son, Dean, lives in Miami and just turned 49 years old. There was a time, several years ago, after he had had an automobile accident, that doctors discovered some damage to his heart. They had to open his chest cavity and work directly on his heart to repair the damage. The operation was successful, but, when he woke up he asked his nurse if he could speak to the blond headed lady who operated on him.

"Who was the last person you talked to before you went to sleep?" asked the nurse.

"I think it was the anesthesiologist," answered Dean.

"Then how would you know what the doctor looked like? Since it was an emergency surgery, you would have had whatever doctor that was available," said the nurse.

"Well, I will tell you, but you probably will not believe me," answered Dean. "After I went to sleep, I found myself 'coming up out of my body' and I sort of hovered over my bed and watched what was going on." Dean described several details of the operation that surprised the nurse.

"But, how would you even know that your doctor was a woman? And how would you know that she had blond hair?" asked the nurse. "In surgery, everyone is totally covered in white from head to toe."

"Well, after the operation I watched her as she went into the adjoining room, where the sink is, and she took off her white jacket and her face mask and her white cap. She washed her hands and that is where I saw her blond hair."

The nurse was amazed and said that he was quite right in every detail and that she would ask the doctor to come see him.

Later that day, the doctor DID come in. She said, "the nurse said you wanted to see 'the blond headed lady who operated on you'. I asked her how you knew that I was a 'blond headed lady' the way that I was all covered up. She wouldn't tell me because she said that I needed to hear it from you myself, so here I am!"

So Dean said, "First of all, I want to thank you, because I feel like you saved my life." Then he told her the same story that he had told the nurse. Then he told her something that he had NOT told the nurse. "I also heard you keep saying, over and over, 'stay with me! Come on, now, stay with me!

Don't go! Stay with me!'. I think it really helped me come back when I heard you."

This admission seemed to startle the doctor. It almost seemed as if she had to check her footing. Then she said, "I WAS saying that! I often say that when the patient is in a dangerous situation. But I NEVER say it out loud! The only thing I ever say out loud as I am concentrating on the surgery, is to ask for whatever instruments I need to continue. I was saying that only in my own mind! And some how you HEARD THAT! "

"Yes Ma'am. I heard it just like I am hearing you now."

"Mr. Hancock, I have heard similar stories before and read about them in books, but this is the first time it has ever happened to me personally. I certainly DO believe you and I thank you for telling me."

My son's heart is fine now. But, by his own testimony, there was a period of time in which he was clinically dead on the operating table. Since he DID survive the operation, we would consider his experience a "near death" experience. His "out of body" experience and the things that he was able to report about the surgery, even though he was totally sedated, are, to me, evidence that he was not just imagining the experience. I have talked with him a number of times about it and I do not believe that he has embellished his story. He is convinced that, although he did not experience some of the things experienced by others, like moving through a tunnel or seeing relatives who have "gone on before", he was definitely experiencing some of what Heaven is like and that he will never, ever, have the least bit of fear of death again.

I have read and heard of many " near death" experiences, but when it comes from your own child, it carries more weight. I am more convinced than ever that Heaven is much more than just a hope based on the testimony of the Bible, as important as that is. It is an existing reality that can be and is experienced by people today. I hope that you will go on line and look up "Near Death Experiences". It will strengthen your own faith as it has strengthened mine.

Prayer: Father, thank you for this little "window" that you have left open so that we can see just a little glimpse of what Heaven is like.

CHAPTER 9: OUR IMPERFECTIONS

There is a song of yesteryear called "My Funny Valentine". It was a cute little song that listed the short comings of the boy's girl friend but quickly added "but don't change a hair for me, not if you care for me – stay little Valentine – stay. Each day is Valentine's day!" In other words, it was the imperfections that endeared his sweetheart to him. Imperfections.

Are any of you stamp collectors? I do not know a lot about stamps, but I do know that a perfectly printed new stamp is probably worth the price you paid for It and nothing more, but a stamp that has imperfections could be like money in the bank. Just as an example, there was a stamp issued in May of 1918 that had a picture of a Curtis "Jenny" airplane on it. The "Jenny" was the plane that many of our American aviators trained in for World War I. When the stamp came out, a few were misprinted with the picture of the airplane upside down. A single stamp was later sold at auction for $977,500 in 2007. In 2005 a block of 4 of the same "upside down Jenny" stamps was sold for 2.7 million dollars. Imperfections.

I believe the same is true of rare coins. Are any of you coin collectors? A penny is usually worth a penny, right. But a 14 year old boy found a very special penny one day. It was a 1943 copper penny. It was not supposed to even exist. We were at war in 1943 and copper was crucial to the war effort. So, pennies were made of steel. Remember those steel pennies? But someone slipped up one day and made a few of them out of copper. The copper penny that the little boy found later sold for $75,000 at auction. It was the imperfection and the rarity that gave it value.

Along those same lines, there was a song that was very popular several years ago by a British singer named Joe Cocker. The name of the song was "You Are So Beautiful". It was a beautiful song but Joe Cocker's recording became exceptionally popular largely, I believe, because of an imperfection. As Joe sang that beautiful phrase for the very last time - "You are so beautiful to me..", his voice cracked on the very last word and it emphasized the deep emotions that the singer was feeling as he sang. The effect was to give an added emotional impact to the song. It was an imperfection that added greatly to the value of the song.

Now, all of these examples illustrate to me something that I believe about how God feels about you and me. Paul also touches on this in II Cor. 12. Paul said "Lest I should be exalted above measure, there was given to me 'a thorn in the flesh'.....For this thing I besought the Lord thrice, that it might depart from me. And the Lord said unto me ' My grace is sufficient for thee; for my strength is made perfect in weakness.'" Paul had been given an imperfection. But, as a result of the way God felt about Paul's imperfection, Paul said, "Therefore I will glory in my infirmities, that the power of Christ may rest upon me."

Paul was saying that God does not mind our imperfections and our short comings, for these imperfections allow God's grace and power to really shine. He loves us, not IN SPITE OF OUR IMPERFECTIONS but, in a sense, BECAUSE OF OUR IMPERFECTIONS. In a way, God is saying the same thing as the song, "My Funny Valentine" is saying, "Don't change a hair for me, not if you care for me, stay little Valentine stay". To say it in a little different way, I think God is saying, "My child, I want to help you to always be becoming the best self that you can be. But I want you to continue to be who you are. Don't try to be someone else. Be yourself, warts and all and I will love you just as I created you to be."

I don't know how you feel about yourself. Do you live with a sense of guilt or a feeling that you have never quite come up to what you think God wants you to be? Or do you feel good about who you are? Do you like who you are? If I am right and I believe I am, God loves you just as you are and just as He is leading you to become day by day. When you think about your children, you love them just as they are, with all of their imperfections. That is exactly the way God feels about you and me.

CHAPTER 10: CARMENA AND GOD

My son, Dean, lives in Miami and knows that I am always looking for a Devotional Story, so he has furnished me several stories that I have used in the past. Last night he called and said, "Dad, I have another story for you!"

That story is what I want to share with you this morning. It is about Carmena and God. It is another example, I believe, of how God intervenes in our lives in order to bless us. Carmena is a "Cleaning Lady" that my son has known for many years because she cleans the homes of several of Dean's friends and he has seen her many times in those homes. They have become close friends. Carmena came from Brazil as a young woman. She is a very independent lady with a very strong work ethic. She works 7 days a week, often cleaning 2 or 3 homes each day. As a result, her reputation as a cleaning lady has reached far and wide. Dean had not seen her for a long time until she saw him at Publix last night and said, "Dean, I have something that I want to tell you!"

They found a place to sit down and Carmena told this story. A man called her and said that he was the "House Manager" for a man who needs a cleaning lady. "He has heard how efficient and dependable you are and he is prepared to offer you a really generous salary. The only stipulation is that you have your nails manicured and your hair done regularly. You will also have to wear a uniform, which he will provide."

"No!" said Carmena.

The man was dumbfounded. "What do you mean? 'No'.You will at least talk to him?"

"Why should I talk with him? I will NOT manicure my nails when they go into bleach? I do my own hair, no one else touches it! And why would I wear a uniform to get sweaty and dirty? No!"

"Will you at least talk with him?"

"Who is this man?" asked Carmena.

"I can not tell you now."

"Then I will not talk with him now!"

"OK. He is Rocky Contino*!" (This is a psuedo name for a real person who is a world famous singer from Porto Rico who is now an adult but has been making records since he was 12 years old and was singing with a famous boys' popular singing group.)

The gentleman finally got Carmena to agree to

talk with the singer at his mansion. He sent a car for her. She saw this huge white mansion and still turned down the offer. She felt that she would rather continue with her present customers. The generous financial offer did not change her answer.

The singer, himself, called her but she turned him down a second time. The singer was not used to being told "No". Carmena thought no more about it.

8 years later, Carmena became sick. Her doctor sent her to an Oncologist. After tests, the Oncologist told her that she had liver cancer and that she would die within about 3 months unless she had surgery. The only problem was that her meager insurance would not pay but a small part of the bill, which would be about $48,000 for the operation and about $20,000 for medicines, therapies, and extended nursing. "There is no way I can pay that! I will just have to die!" She ran from the doctor's office with her eyes half blind with tears.

She got on the elevator and there was a man there. He asked her what was the matter and, in her desperation, she spilled the whole story. He enveloped her in his arms and spoke comforting words to her. She was glad to receive comfort, even from a stranger. She had no idea who the man was but he told her that "everything is going to be alright." She took this as a way to make her feel better and thought no more about it. She went home and cried in despair. Later that day the Oncologist called her and said that the surgery was set for a certain time and date, if Carmena could be there on that date.

"I have already told you that I can not pay!" said Carmena.

"The total bill has been taken care of," replied the Oncologist. "All of your expenses all through your recovery and therapy will be covered no matter how long it takes," assured the Oncologist.

"I don't understand," cried Carmena. "Who would do this?" Carmena was dumbfounded.

"Your Benefactor," said the Oncologist.

"I will NOT do it unless you tell me who!" said an independent Carmena.

"In that case I guess I will have to tell you. It is Mr. Rocky Contino. He wants to remain anonymous as much as possible."

Carmena was almost speechless but managed to say, "But why?"

"I am afraid that you will have to ask him that question," answered the Oncologist.

Carmena did go through with the surgery. The

MY BEST TO YOU FOREVER

surgery was 12 hours long and Mr. Contino was outside in the waiting room the whole time. Carmena knew he was there because the nature of the surgery required that she be conscious during the whole operation. She saw him before and afterward in the waiting room. She told Dean that she had no fear during the whole operation. It was as though God was "hugging her" with a warm, loving hug the whole time. Rocky also sat with Carmena several times during her recovery. When Carmena went home, Rocky sent his own nurse to stay with her every day. She even showed Carmena how to make a Protein milk shake to hasten her recovery. At some point during Rocky's visits, Carmena managed to ask him the question, "Why?"

"Several reasons, I guess," answered Rocky. "You are the first person that ever told me 'no' twice. I guess I admired you because you 'can't be bought'. Also, even though I have been rich since I was 12, I knew what it was like to be poor before that. My family could never have afforded such an operation as you had to have. Also, Carmena, what it is costing me isn't going to hurt me and I hope it's going to help you a lot. There is one thing that I DO want you to know. I had no reason to be in that building or in that elevator that day. But the moment that you got on the elevator and

49

told me your story, I knew that I had been led there to do exactly what I did. I honestly believe that 'it was meant for me to be there!'"

After telling her story, Carmena said to my son, " Do you think God does things like that?"

"Do you mean do I think that God was intervening to give you some help? I sure do, Carmena. He has done it for me many times in my life! I could probably name half a dozen times without even thinking about it. And I can't help but feel, Carmena, that Rocky was one of the 'Angels on earth' that God counts on to 'get things done." Although the surgery was in June, the Nurse is still coming every day, this is August, to make a protein shake for Carmena!

To you who have heard this true story, I hope that you have had times when you were aware of God helping you in a special way through events that happened or from someone coming to your aid when you least expected it. I hope that you did not mark it off as a fortunate coincidence or mere chance. I hope that you can see that God was at work. Carmena and Rocky and Dean definitely feel that God was working in that elevator on that special afternoon. I believe it too.

Prayer: Thank you Father for loving us enough to get involved in our lives. Help us to love you more because of that. In Jesus' name, Amen.

* The names "Carmena" and "Rocky Contino" are fictitious names for the real people involved.

CHAPTER 11: GOD'S VOICE

There is a passage of Scripture in 1 Kings, Chapter 19 of the Old Testament in which the Prophet Elijah was in despair because Queen Jezebel was planning to kill him. He wanted to hear the voice of God. The scripture says that there was a mighty wind but that God was NOT in the wind. Then there was an earthquake but God was NOT in the earthquake. After that there was a fire but God was NOT in the fire. But, after the fire, there was a still, small voice. It WAS God.

When God speaks, even today, it is usually in a small quiet voice. When I gave this devotional originally, I used a small, 2 inch by 2 inch music box mechanism that played "Silent Night". I wound it up and let it play. I could barely hear it as I held it in my hand, but the audience could not hear it at all. But I held it up to a wall and they could hear it perfectly. I placed it on the piano and they heard it. I even placed it on a small wooden box and on the back of a metal pan and they heard it fine.

Each sounding board had just a bit different tone but each was a good "resonator" for the small voice that the music player had by itself. That is a perfect example of how God's still, small voice needs a "resonator" if today's society is ever going to hear what God has to say to them. God has chosen several resonators. THE BEAUTY OF NATURE is one such resonator. Many people hear God speaking to them in rainbows and mountain grandeur and moonlight nights.

Another such resonator is LIFE'S EVENTS, 'GOOD' AND 'BAD'. God sometimes gets people's attention in an accident that almost happens or in one that DOES happen, in an almost fatal illness, or in the loss or almost loss of a loved one.

But the sort of resonator that God depends on most of all is you and me and other folks like us. We who have been privileged to experience God in our lives are able to "pass that experience on to other folks" in simple acts of kindness or in words which convey what our experience has been with God. A friend is sad and God's still, small voice gives us the words to say to that friend and he or she hears words of comfort from God, resonated through us just as surely as that wall or that piano or that little box made the voice of "silent night" audible to us just now.

A child who is afraid hears confidence in his parent's words but he is really hearing the still, small comforting voice of God. A young Christian is experiencing an unfamiliar season of doubting his new faith and you share with him how you have traveled through times of doubt and have come safely back to faith in God, strengthened rather than weakened by that experience. He has heard the wee, small voice of God, amplified in your honestly shared experience.

You can be God's resonator every day with every smile that you give and with every time you hold the door for someone following you into a department store. You act as such every time you say "thank you" for a kindness done to you and every time you express a word of encouragement to a person "having a bad time". Every time you exhibit a positive, grateful, loving spirit in ANY way, you are being a "resonator" for God's voice so that your family, your friends, and even strangers might hear the voice of God.

Being a "resonator" is much like C.P.R – the technique for keeping a person's heart beating after he has experienced "heart arrest". You see, even a Cardiologist who has had heart arrest, can not help himself. But a school boy who has learned how to do C.P.R can save the Cardiologist's life. So it is with our being a "resonator". Your Pastor might be having a discouraging time in which he can not seem to hear God's voice of encouragement, and your words saying that his sermon was "just what you needed" might be just what he needed to hear the strengthening voice of God to his spirit!

CHAPTER 12: O HENRY'S CHRISTMAS GIFT

There is a Christmas story, written by an author of bygone days whose name was O Henry. In this story there was a husband, Jim, and a wife, Della. They lived at a time in our history when the economy was in poor straits. Jim had been making $30.00 a week and this, because of the economy, had been reduced to $20.00. His wife did not work. They lived in an $8.00 a week flat, so that just left $12.00 for all of their other expenses.

Now it was Christmas Eve and neither one of them had a present for the other. Della counted her money and had just $1.87 to her name. That was not much to buy a nice present for her husband. She thought of what she might take to the pawn shop, but there simply was nothing. She had beautiful long, brown hair that went to below her knees when she combed it out. What she really wanted to give to Jim was this. His prize possession was a gold pocket watch that had originally belonged to his grandfather and then his father. It had been passed down to Jim when his father died. This beautiful watch, however, was attached to Jim's belt by an old strand of leather, which Jim always tried to hide with his hand whenever he pulled out his watch to check the time. Della really wanted to get him a nice gold watch chain that would be worthy of his watch. But she certainly could not do that with $1.87.

She knew that a local wig maker would pay on the spot for hair that would be suitable for wigs. Della put on her old coat and a wool cap and went out into the weather. She went to the wig maker and asked her what she would give for her hair. Della removed her cap and the wig maker almost drooled at the sight. "I will give you $20.00 for the whole length," she said. "That is a week's wages for my Jim," thought Della. "Do it now!" she said to the wig lady.

Della went immediately to the shops on main street. She felt positively bald, and she wondered if Jim would still think she was pretty. But she found a beautiful watch chain, solid gold, for $21.00. She brought back $.87 in her purse. She had the chain safely folded in her purse also.

When she got home it was not quite time for Jim to be home so she got out the curling iron, heated it on the stove, and began curling the short locks of her hair into ringlets, all over her head. She was very fearful that Jim would hate what she had done. He was late getting home and she began to worry.

Finally she heard Jim open their front door, then she saw his smiling face turn into a look that she had never seen on her husband before. It was not disappointment and it was not surprise. It was a look that was too complex for Della to interpret. Finally he said, "What have you done, Della?"

"I...I wanted to get you a nice present for Christmas, Jim. I knew how much you wanted a watch chain to replace that old strand of leather. I didn't have any money, so I sold my hair to the wig lady and bought you this! I can grow more hair, Dear. Now, let me see your watch so that I can put this chain on it!"

He looked at the beautiful chain and paused for a long time. "Hon, I sold my watch at the pawn shop and got you these!" He opened his hand and there were two beautiful tortoise shell combs that he had seen her wish for a hundred times as they had looked in the shop windows together. She looked at the beautiful combs in admiration for a few moments and then they were both speechless as the full weight of the irony of their situation settled into their minds.

"You loved me enough to cut the hair that you have not cut since childhood in order to give me a present, Hon?" said Jim, trying to absorb the full impact of this act of devotion.

"And you loved me enough to sell....to sell your grandfather's gold watch, to buy me these precious combs?" marveled Della.

There were tears in the eyes of both of these loving people. "I will grow my hair back and use these combs every day, my Darling!" said Della.

And I will save every week until I can redeem my watch from Frank at the pawn shop, Della. I will go by the day after Christmas and plead for him to put my watch away until I have paid him back with interest," said Jim. "Then I can put this beautiful chain on it."

This story suggests to me that our Christmas gifts can all represent our love if we will just make our love for each person foremost in our gift buying. As you decide what you are going to give each person think briefly about what this person means to you. As you wrap the present, think of the wrapping paper as being your love wrapping around the present. As you present the present, think of it as representing your love for the person. It might sound a bit strange to you but just thinking in these terms as you deal with present giving, will make a lot of difference!

CHAPTER 13: KNOWING OR LIVING BY FAITH

TEXT: John 20:29 "Jesus saith unto him,'Thomas, because you have seen me you have believed. Blessed are they that have NOT seen, and yet have believed'". Jesus had appeared to the other disciples   after His resurrection, but Thomas was not present. When they told Thomas that Jesus had been back to see them, he did not believe them. He said that he would not believe unless he could put his finger in Jesus' nail scarred hand and put his hand in Jesus' side. Then Jesus appeared again when Thomas was there and invited Thomas to touch him. It was then that Thomas said, "My Lord and My God."

It was right after that when Jesus said the words of our text: "Thomas, because you have seen me you have believed. Blessed are they that have NOT seen, and yet have believed".

One of my strongest desires is to KNOW, rather than just believe, hope, or have faith. There IS a difference. Even though Thomas basically trusted the other disciples, he did NOT believe them when they made such a preposterous statement that "Jesus was alive". He had seen Jesus killed. He KNEW that Jesus was dead. I think that with all of us, even though we WANT to believe and we DO believe, as much as we can. But in all belief there is probably that one little bit of doubt, that realization that believing is never quite the same as KNOWING. When Thomas had seen Jesus, he did not just believe. He knew that Jesus was alive again. You see, I would like to actually KNOW, just like Thomas knew, instead of just having faith and hope.

God could have arranged things differently – that is, He could have arranged for each of us to have a Pentecostal kind of experience, foe instance, tongues of fire, seeing Christ face to face, touching his hand and side, or even an experience as dramatic as Paul had on the Damascus Road. If each of us could have had such an experience, it would certainly have made it a lot easier for each of us. That is the way I probably would have arranged it if God had left it up to me.

But then again, I would probably have arranged it so that everyone would be the optimum physical size instead of so many of us being fat. But then we would not have been required to use personal discipline. I probably would have given everyone strong muscles and good cardiovascular systems. But then we would not have had to do exercise and aerobics. And, I probably would have let everyone come to earth knowing all about God and Heaven and how to live a perfect life – knowing all of it without ever having any doubts about any of it.

But, if God had left it up to me and I had done it that way, I believe God would probably have called me over to the side and said, "Don, you are missing the point of why I send folks to earth in the first place. You see, the reason I let people come to earth in the first place is for them to learn the things that they need to know and do the things that they need to do in order to be the strong, mature spiritual beings that I want them to be."

"They would not really appreciate their strong bodies if they just have them given to them without their own effort. But, if they have to exercise and eat right, etc, then they will be growing strong will power in the process. And if you let them have all knowing automatically without them having to learn it the hard way, then they will miss learning the discipline of self control. So, what would be the purpose of them going to earth in the first place?"

"In the same way, if you were to let them go to earth knowing and remembering everything about Heaven and if there was no need for faith and hope, then that would be exactly like letting their brains know without learning and letting their bodies be strong and healthy without exercise. You would be expecting them to be strong spiritually without the spiritual exercise that we call 'faith'. It just could not happen. That is why my Son, Jesus told Thomas, 'Blessed are those who have not seen my hands and my side but yet have believed."

So, all of you who seek to follow God, be content with not KNOWING so completely that you can discard faith and hope. Yes, it would be just like being in Heaven on earth. But you would be missing the real reason that God sent you to earth in the first place – to grow your spiritual life! It is the same reason that you take your body to the gym and your mind to school. God sends your spirits to earth to grow. And your spirits can not grow unless it exercises faith. That's just the way it is.

Yes, God DID give the disciples at that first Easter much more evidence and stronger signs than He gives any of us today. Maybe it was because He knew that it was going to be very difficult for those early followers to stand up to the opposition of the Jewish leaders and the pagan society in which they lived. But whatever the reason that He gave them an abundance of miracles and He makes us get along mostly with just faith and hope, we can trust Him to know what is best. So, let us pray for a stronger faith, a stronger hope, and whatever miracles and signs He might see fit to give us.

Prayer: Dear Father, help us to be content, not with what we want for ourselves but with what YOU want FOR us. In Jesus' name, Amen.

CHAPTER 14; CAST YOUR BREAD ON THE WATER

As you know, my son, Dean, lives in Miami and has, from time to time, heard some interesting stories from his friends. I wanted to share 3 of these true stories this morning because they illustrate how doing acts of kindness can bring unusual blessings beyond what could be imagined at the time the act was done.

The first one is about a fashion model that Dean knows named Paulina. Dean did some fashion modeling on the side when he was in school. He is 6' 4" tall and there were not many male models that tall. Paulina was a 6' model and so, every time Paulina did any modeling at a fashion show and needed a male escort on the stage, they would call Dean. At each fashion show there was a lot of "back stage' time and so they did a lot of talking. Paulina told her story to Dean. She was born in Poland and was orphaned as a young child. The orphan homes in Poland at the time were deplorable, with each child, regardless of age, kept in a metal bed with cage like sides. There was very little individual care and most of the children just cried all day. A traveling American couple "rescued" Paulina and brought her to their home in Miami. She grew up in good schools and with all of her needs met. She was beautiful and she became a fashion model. She married a local lawyer and she told him about her days in Poland. They later went for a vacation in Poland and she took him to see the home that she resided in when rescued. The conditions were just as bad as she had experienced as a child. She and her husband decided to begin a Foundation for the purpose of rescuing as many of those children as they could. At the time that he talked to her, they had already found homes in the US for 20 of those children. The couple who adopted Paulina blessed many more children as a result of their act of compassion.

There is another story which I might have told you before some time ago but it bears repeating. There was a well known automobile dealership in Miami called Abraham.................. Mr. Abraham and his wife were philanthropists who would regularly travel to third world countries and visit orphanages with food and supplies. One day they were going in a taxi from an orphanage to their hotel and they saw a little girl, too young to be by herself, walking on the street in a tattered dress. They asked their guide, "Why is that child walking the streets at her age?" The guide answered, "She has no family, no home, no one, Mr. Abraham."

"Why is she not in an orphan's home," asked Mrs. Abraham.

"There is only so much room, Sir", answered the guide.

"How would I go about adopting that little girl?" asked Mr. Abraham.

"I believe you would just sign a few papers and pay a fee," said the guide. After conferring with his wife, they went to the authorities and negotiated the child's adoption. This wandering girl with the tattered dress became the daughter of the Abrahams. She now owns, among other things, the property that houses the Miami International Airport. Miami International pays their monthly rent to this former orphan, whose life was changed forever by the compassion of two people who had the means to make a difference.

The last story is not quite as important or dramatic, but is still interesting. Dean has a friend who is a male flight attendant. He also happens to be a big tennis fan. On one of his flights, he noticed that Martina Navratilova was sitting in the Coach section. She was flying "stand by" and

Coach was the only ticket available. He recognized her because she was the number 1 women's tennis player in the world at that time. Since he had several empty seats in "First Class", he said, "Miss Navratilova, we do have a seat in First Class if you will allow me to move you there."

"Well, that is so nice. Thank you very much." He removed what she had in the "over head" and showed her to her new seat. In the course of the move they "talked tennis" and she realized that he was a "real fan". She gave him credentials that would allow him a "box seat" at all of her matches. Now that she has retired he still has a pass for box seats at all the major matches. Recently he sat behind Prince William and Kate. His random act of kindness certainly had a far reaching benefit, and he is very glad that he went a little bit out of his way to be helpful.

I wanted to share these stories just to remind you that when you do any act of kindness, large or small, we really have no way of knowing how large or small it will turn out after God places His hand on it. Nor do we have any way of knowing how far it will reach or how many people it will bless before its influence is completed.

Prayer: Dear Father, help us to be willing to do any act of kindness that you place in our heart to do,

CHAPTER 15: "INDEPENDENCE DAY "

Tomorrow is July 4, our country's Day of Independence. There should be two programs either tonight or tomorrow night that I would encourage you to see. One is the program that always originates from our nation's capital grounds and the other comes from the First Baptist Church of Columbia, S.C. Both programs will make you proud that you are an American.

As we approach Independence Day, we are reminded of a very famous day of independence in the past, the day that the Prodigal Son left his home. He must have dreamed of that day for a long time before he finally got up his courage to ask his father for his part of his inheritance so that he could "be free" to search for his future. As you remember, it was a case of an independence "gone wrong".

In a way, the story of the Prodigal is the story of "Everyman". We should not blame the Prodigal Son too harshly. I believe that God places in every little baby that is born, a desire for independence. If we did not have that built in desire for independence, a baby would never want to leave the security of breast feeding or the baby bottle. He would never learn to grasp a spoon and try to eat food that has to be chewed with effort.

The desire for independence is what leads the teen ager to long for the day he can drive a car and then for the day that he can get a job and move to his own apartment and then marry and have a family of his own. And this is all part of God's plan. The Prodigal was following that inner urge but apparently he made a few wrong choices along that path.

All of us have probably had a wonderful life of independence. We have had marriages, families, and careers. As was the case with the Prodigal, we might have even made some mistakes along the way. If that is the case, please do not feel too badly about it. I believe that our mistakes, along with our wise choices, are all a part of what it takes for us to grow and mature and become more independent.

Now, many of us in our department are facing the prospect of having our long held independence modified in one way or another. A neighbor that Finetta and I are very close to, faced losing her driver's license several years ago. That was hard. Some of you have already faced that. All of us will if we live long enough. But now that neighbor is facing the necessity of giving up her private home and going to some sort of assisted living arrangement.

All of us face the possibility of that sort of loss of independence, unless we are fortunate enough to be able to live with extended family. But let me remind you of the progression of the story of the Prodigal. In the beginning he enjoyed several years of independence. But then, because of poor choices, he found that his independence had left him in a state of need. He longed to go back to his father's house, not as a son, but just as a hired servant. But he was surprised to find out that his future was much brighter than he had expected. He was fully loved and accepted as a son by his father. I believe that our neighbor might find that her future might have far more happiness than she expects. I believe that, as each of us meets the challenges in our future, we too might find that the changes that we experience might be happier than we expect. But whatever happens, we should do all that we can to be grateful to those who help us, to be as kind and good natured as our bodies and minds will allow us to be, and try to be good servants of God as long as He gives us life and breath.

But no matter what our immediate future holds for us on this earth, the ultimate news is GOOD news for each of us. We might find ourselves worried, as was the Prodigal as he dreaded going back to his father. Even though we have heard wonderful things about Heaven, we might be just a little worried whenever we think about the end of our life. But, just as the Prodigal son found out, we need not have worried. Everything is going to be fine!

Let Us Pray: Dear Father. As we face our individual futures, help us to have complete confidence that we are in Your hands and that you love us even more than we love ourselves. In Jesus' name. Amen.

CHAPTER 16: POLITICS

I have entitled this devotional "Politics" but don't worry, I am NOT going to be controversial. This is a political year. You might say, "what year isn't?" and you would be right. Life itself is political, in a sense. It is full of decisions that effect our lives directly. This is a presidential election year and the choice seems to be between Donald Trump and Hillary Clinton. My wife and I have tried to be good stewards of our "freedom to choose" and so we have listened endlessly to opinions on both sides and have followed everything from the beginnings, through the primaries and now as we face the elections. As always there are several opinions. Some folks think the best choice is obvious. Others do not even want to vote because they can not stand to choose either candidate. Others will simply refuse to vote. But that is the way it has always been with politics.

I almost called this devotional "LIFE IS LIKE A SOUP". "How can there be any similarity between soup and politics?" you might ask. We shall see shortly. We eat a lot of soup at our house.

My wife and I have our specialties. She makes a wonderful, hearty vegetable soup, usually slow cooked in the "crock pot" with roast beef, potatoes, tomatoes, green beans, and other veggies. My soup is usually made of yellow and/or green squash, potatoes, onions, carrots, and whatever meat is available – sausage, beef, ham, or whatever. Our soups usually turn out tasty but often different, some times even problematical. Last week I had no squash and so I looked in the freezer for "whatever". I found what I thought were "sugar snap peas", those wonderful little short things that you can just toss into soup or the frying pan, shell and all, and they come out tender and sweet. These turned out to be "other than sugar snap peas" and after I had tossed in about two cups of these "impersonators" and cooked the soup for an hour, the pea shells seemed to be made of hard plastic. I ended up going through the whole pot of soup and hand picking these culprits out, a cup at a time. In my consternation, I forgot to even add carrots and onions, but I added cream corn and, in the end, my "problematical" soup tasted different but quite good.

So, what does soup have to do with politics? We who place a lot of importance on the Bible and on Bible history, know that the Old Testament is absolutely full of "politics", from one end to the other. Although it is about Kings rather than Presidents, the story of Old Testament times is a story about the "ends and outs" of politics. Choosing Kings, dealing with other nations, wars, intrigues, errors in judgment, outright disasters. All of that and more is the substance of the Old Testament stories.

The best of the Kings were only human and made grave errors. David, who was a man who was chosen by God, took another man's wife and saw to it that the husband was killed in battle. Solomon, who was supposed to be so full of wisdom, made terrible blunders. What came out of all of this was the "soup" that we call "the Hebrew People", which was the "soup starter" for the "soup" that we call "Christianity". In a sense, God was making the soup, and He made it out of the ingredients that He had available at the time, some of which were "problematical". But another name for what I have called "God's soup making" is "Life".

You and I have been given the privilege of being in "God's soup" which we call "our life time". In a sense, we are "co-soup makers" with God. God is making the soup called "American History" with the help of you and me. He and we are making this soup out of whatever ingredients we find available. The outcome of this soup might seem "good" or "bad" or "so so" or "could have used a bit more salt". It might even be, as my last soup, "problematical".

Whatever happens in the November elections will probably be given one of the above labels by those who label history. But, in the end, it will be the soup that we helped make. It will be the soup that God officiated in the making. As with God's other creations, as the Bible reports, He will, hopefully, call it "Good!" And when we take leave of this life on earth and go back to our Heavenly Father, He will, hopefully, say to us, "Well done, thou good and faithful servant", as I hope He will also say of Donald Trump and Hillary and Bill Clinton, and Kind David, and King Solomon, and others – all of whom were, perhaps, "problematical".

I said that I would not be controversial and you might feel that I stepped over the line on that last statement. You are a soup maker along with me and God, so you have as much right to your opinion about what should go into the soup as I do, and I respect and encourage that right.

Let us pray: Dear Father, help us to take our life and the life of our Nation seriously, but not too seriously, knowing that beneath and above and around all of life is Your loving and forgiving Presence. In Jesus' name. Amen.

CHAPTER 17: SONGS OF THE PAST WE NEED TODAY

There were some songs we sang in the past that reminded us of values that we needed then. Perhaps we need to look again at some of those values. Such values as peace and love and the grace of God, and the danger of losing those values. I am not a pessimist, but these are difficult times that we are living in today. We are in danger in our national life of replacing Statesmanship with a "whatever it takes to win" kind of politics. Violence seems to be replacing respect and civility as a way of dealing with disagreements. Racial problems are still with us after all these years, and love for neighbors seems to be woefully lacking. This song recognized those problems years ago. Maybe we need to sing it again today.

IF I HAD A HAMMER. This song was sung by Peter, Paul, and Mary, by Pete Seeger and many others. I hope you still remember it. It goes like this:

"If I had a hammer, I'd hammer in the morning, I'd hammer in the evening, All over this land.

I'd hammer out danger, I'd hammer out a warning, I'd hammer out love between my brothers and my sisters, All over this land".

"If I had a bell, I'd ring it in the morning, I'd ring it in the evening, All over this land.
I'd ring out danger, I'd ring out a warning, I'd ring out love between my brothers and my sisters,
All over this land".

"If I had a song, I'd sing it in the morning, I'd sing it in the evening, All over this land.
I'd sing out danger, I'd sing out a warning, I'd sing out love between my brothers and my sisters,
All over this land".

"Well I got a hammer, And I got a bell, And I got a song to sing, all over this land.
It's the hammer of Justice, It's the bell of Freedom, It's the song about Love between my brothers and my sisters, All over this land".

"It's the hammer of Justice, It's the bell of Freedom, It's the song about Love between my brothers and my sisters, All over this land".

So, today, we find that we are, again, in a time of unrest. It is again a time when we need to ask God to help us give freedom to those who do not feel free and justice to those who feel unjustly treated. No, we don't need a hammer and we don't even need a bell. But we sure do need for God to heal our country by giving us love between our brothers and out sisters, all over this land.

THIS LAND IS YOUR LAND was a song of patriotism and appreciation of our country. It was written by Woody Guthrie in the 1940's, The Great Depression was still going on and it was a time when many people felt abandoned and dispossessed and fearful. This song began with the chorus. Let's look at it together.

CHORUS: "This land is your land, this land is my land, from California to the New York Island, From the Redwood Forest to the Gulf Stream waters, this land was made for you and me".

"As I was walking that ribbon of highway, I saw above me that endless skyway,
I saw below me that golden valley, this land was made for you and me". CHORUS

"I roamed and I rambled and I followed my footsteps to the sparkling sands of her diamond deserts, While all around me a voice was sounding this land was made for you and me". Chorus.

When we sing that song it just seems natural to follow it with another song that never goes out of style. It was important in the 40's, the 50's, the 60's, and is still important today.

GOD BLESS AMERICA

"God bless America, land that I love, stand beside her and guide her through the night with the light from above.
From the mountains to the prairies to the oceans white with foam,
God bless America, my home sweet home, God bless America, my home sweet home".

This song adds its own version of appreciation of our country but adds the belief that it's goodness and it's welfare depend on the blessings of God, it's Creator.

During the early Seventies, I remember that there was a very popular recording, played often on the radio. It was a simple, straight forward, and unashamed rendition, by Judy Collins, of AMAZING GRACE. We know it but let's look at the words. We need these words today.

"Amazing Grace how sweet the sound that saved a wretch like me. I once was lost but now I am found, was blind but now I see".

"Twas grace that taught my heart to fear and grace my fears relieved. How precious did that grace appear the hour I first believed".

Through many dangers, toils, and snares I have already come, tis grace hath bsrought me safe thus far,   And grace will lead me home.

"When we've been there ten thousand years,

bright, shining as the sun. We've no less days to sing God's praise than when we first begun".

That song reminds us that, not only does our country need God's blessing and grace, but we need it personally ourselves.

Let us pray: Dear Father, help us to realize that if this country allows violence to take the place of neighborly love, and if we allow pure self interest to take the place of love for our country, then we ARE in danger and we do need a WARNING and we do need to hear a song of love between our brothers and our sisters all over this land. In Jesus' name, Amen.

DONALD C. HANCOCK

CHAPTER 18: GROWING OLDER

I went with my wife to get her weekly "hair care" this morning. I also got my little bit of hair trimmed by the same lady while my wife's hair was drying. As the lady was cutting my hair, I noticed pictures of her great grand child. It was a very young, small baby that could almost fit into its father's hand. I thought to myself, "Was I ever actually that young and that small?"

I am about to become 84 years old and when someone asks me how I am I often jokingly say, "Well, in my garden my plants come up fresh and green, then they ripen, they shrivel, they wither, and die. I think I am somewhere between 'shrivel' and 'wither'." It is so. Nothing works as well as it did a few years ago. But, on the other hand, I am still able to walk for 30 minutes four or five times a week and I just began going to an exercise class three times a week where we work with barbells for an hour. It is called 'Body Pump', and most of the other folks in the class are between 20 and 50 years old. I keep up with them pretty well.

So yes, I look like I am somewhere between shriveled and withered, but I am not dead yet. Yet, when I am dead, that will be OK too. As the Apostle Paul said, "To be absent from the body (dead) is to be present with the Lord". So, I am in a win/win situation. I am NOT as young or as agile as I used to be. But there are compensations. I am more mature than I used to be. I also feel that my spirit is more mature than it used to be. I feel that, with every year that has been added that I am also a little more experienced in my spiritual life. I feel closer to God. I feel that I know God better. I seem to have more patience, less anxiety, and less fear. In many ways I have gained more with my aging than I have lost by not being young anymore.

Would I like to have a young body again, housing the knowledge and maturity that I have gained? That is an interesting question. I have heard people say that they would like that. If God were to ask me to do that for Him, I would certainly say, "yes", but only because He asked me to do it. It would not be because the idea appeals to me.

Yes, there is a part of me that would like to continue my ministry of writing for a few more years. I am actually enjoying this ministry more than I enjoyed being a Pastor or a Chaplain. But I must also say that there is a part of me that is weary of living in this world. The idea of living another 20 years leaves me cold. I feel as Paul must have felt when he said, "I have fought a good fight, I have finished my course, I have kept the faith", though I do not consider that my life has been a "fight" in any sense.

So, I usually try to write "feel good devotionals", and just maybe this one fails to meet that criteria. But my purpose for writing these thoughts does have a "feel good motive". It is my hope that, if and when you might have a time when you also have such feelings, like "I really would not want to live another 20 years on earth as it is today" or "sometimes I feel like I am ready for God to take me" - when and if those feelings come – then you will know that you are not alone. You will know that there is another fellow traveler that, once in a while, feels the same. I love my life as it is and as it has been. But I get a little homesick to be back again with God.

Prayer: Dear Father, I am ready to stay or ready to go. You know my heart. I want what You want. In Jesus' name, Amen.

DONALD C. HANCOCK

CHAPTER 19: THE HOLY SPIRIT TODAY

You might remember my story of how I lost my wallet and my "Angels" helped me find it exactly where I had put it – in the furnace cabinet of a rental house where I was working. I explained at that time, how I write my prayers on paper and also write my answers to my prayers on the same paper. In other words, I have a conversation with God or my Angels and write both sides of the conversation on the paper.

Well, the older I get the more I will lose things and the more I will have to rely on Heavenly help to find things. I would like to give you two more examples. First, case # 2 of "the lost wallet". Several Sundays ago, we had a visiting Preacher, Rev. David Hull. As I shook hands with him I asked if he was related to Bill Hull. Bill was a Fellow in my class when I was in Seminary years ago. He said that, indeed, Bill Hull was his Father. I asked him about someone else that I knew and he knew him also. I put down my Bible to write down Rev. Hull's email address. I forgot my Bible as I went out to my car. When I got home I had a call from Rev. Chip Reeves, who had left a message. I heard, "Donald, you left your Bible and Sunday Lesson Books at church. They are in my office." "No problem" thought I. "I will pick them up tomorrow."

Later in the afternoon I reached for my wallet. It was not in my pocket or where I usually put it in the house. Finetta, My wife, and I looked all over the house twice and throughout the car twice. So what do I do when I lose something? I ask the Angels. They said very emphatically, "You will find it!" So I kept looking and worrying. We drove over to a rental house where I had gone after church. It wasn't there. I asked the Angels for more help. "You will find it where you put it!" Not much help except to know that I definitely would find it. "When will I find it?" I asked. "Tonight" was the answer. When "tonight" came and I had not found it, I "Fussed" a bit. "You said tonight and I haven't found it yet!" I said. The next morning I decided to go to the church to see if I had dropped it between my car and the church. But, before I left, I decided to listen to the message one more time. I played the message. "Hello, Donald, this is Chip Reeves. You left your Bible, your Sunday School Lesson Books and your Wallet at the church. They are in my office. The Angels were right. It was right where I had left it. I should have listened better and worried less.

The next week end we were going somewhere in the car on Saturday. One of the batteries in a hearing aid quit and I gave the hearing aid to Finetta as I drove so she could put in another battery. I missed her hand and it fell on the floor. No problem, I would find it later. I looked later but did not find it. I asked the Angels. "Look again. It IS in the car" they said. Later that day I unbolted the front seats and looked. I looked over every square inch and did not find it. "Keep looking," they said. "It IS in the car. I unbolted and rebolted the front seats a total of three times without success. Each time, "Keep looking. It IS in the car." I decided that it just had to have fallen out somewhere when we got out of the car. The next day, Sunday, the young lady across the street, who knows about my conversations with my Angels, asked me if I wanted her to look. I said, "I don't see how you can find it if I have looked over every square inch three different times. "And your Angels say it is still in the car?" she asked. "yes, that is what they are saying," said I.

I unbolted the seats for a fourth time. There was a little air conditioner vent under the seat, about 5 inches wide. I had looked in there several times with a flash light. She decided to run something

UNDER the vent in a ½ inch space beneath the vent. There she pulled out 4 lost writing pens AND a hearing aid. Score another one for the angels! It really impressed the young lady from across the street. She already believed in my Angels' help but now she believed even more. I decided that there was a purpose in my delay in finding the hearing aid. I think, perhaps, it was so that my neighbor could also have her faith increased at the same time that mine was strengthened. I really think that the Holy Spirit is still working every day. Not always doing exactly as we want Him to do but still working just the same.

CHAPTER 20: HOW WOULD YOU LABEL YOURSELF?

People love labels. They help us choose the food that we eat. They might even help us choose our friends. If you happen to be conservative, either in faith or in politics, you might choose friends who are also conservative. You might just tend to shy away from someone who is too Fundamentalist on the one hand or too liberal on the other hand.

But I do not know what you will do with me, because I am a Fundamentalist, Conservative, Progressive Liberal Baptist.

I am a Fundamentalist about the things that I consider fundamentals to a good and happy life. To me these fundamentals are: Love, Forgiveness, Acceptance, Compassion, Patience, and Respect. You can probably add a few more. To me they are basic because I believe they are what God is like. We often say that God IS Love. I believe that Love is much more important and powerful than any of us will understand in our short life span. I believe that Christ fully understood the power of Love and that is one of the things that allowed him to do the things that he did. In a sense, Love

DOES make the "world go round" as the song says. In addition, I believe that Forgiveness and Acceptance will trump Rejection in every situation of life where people are involved. I believe that Patience is the reason that God gives us an eternity to live, because He wants us to have plenty of time to learn all the lessons that He has for us.

I believe that God's Respect for each of us is why one of God's greatest gifts to mankind is free will. As much as God wants to help us, He will never force His Will on us. But if everyone on earth were to accept those fundamentals of Love, Forgiveness, Acceptance, Compassion, Patience, and Respect, and try to live by them with God's help, then our problems of violence, crime, terror, and many other problems of our world would disappear as the morning dew. So, yes, I am a fundamentalist.

I am also a Conservative. I would like to bring back and preserve some of the things that worked in our past. Some things that I remember are: Not needing to lock your front door at night, trusting each other because "a person's word was his bond!"

Schools were places where the teacher was totally respected by pupil and parents alike. Little children looked up to a Policeman as though he was "next to God". You knew that, if your children could get a college education you could be pretty sure that they could get a good job soon after graduation. These and other things I remember from the "good old days and I wish it was like that again. That probably makes me a Conservative.

But I am also a Progressive. I am Progressive in the sense that I believe that our knowledge of God has been what the Bible Scholars call Progressive Revelation. The knowledge of God reflected in Samuel's statement to King Saul that God wanted Saul to "Go and smite the Amalekites and destroy all that they have and spare them not, but slay both man and woman, infant and suckling, ox and sheep, camel and ass." Then God was angry because Saul spared the King and brought back a few of the animals to be used as an offering to God.

That view of God is much more primitive and cruel when compared to Jesus' lofty picture of God shown in the parable of the Prodigal Son and the God like father, which, I believe, was Jesus' picture of what God is like. And can you imagine for even a moment hearing Jesus order the total destruction of a city and the slaying of every man, woman, boy, girl, infant and animal in that city. There was a tremendous progression of our view of God during that period. I do not believe that God changed. I believe that man's perception of God changed, or at least the perception of SOME men changed. Some still think that God is cruel and brutal.

When I was a child, I thought it strange that they would say "God is love" and then they would tell a story from the Old Testament about Him calling for murder. But I believed it because "grown ups" said it was so. But I now believe that God has always been loving and forgiving the way Jesus showed him. It was the religious leaders in the Old Testament that had it wrong.

What is more, I do not believe that the progression of God's revelation of Himself and His truths ended with the closing of Bible times. I believe that He continues to show us more of Himself as time goes on. Our knowledge of God IS Progressive. In that sense I am Progressive too!

And, yes, I am Liberal. I am Liberal in the sense that I remember the many ways that Jesus was thought to be "liberal" by the Jewish leaders: Eating and having fellowship with "sinners". Being open to "new ideas" like healing sick people on the Sabbath. Then allowing gentiles to become His followers without becoming Jews first – a very "liberal" idea. I guess that I am Liberal for believing that God is going to let a lot of folks into Heaven that we thought would never be there.

Applying Jesus' liberal thoughts to my life right now, I want to be more liberal in accepting new ideas about worship. I must admit that I tend to be pretty traditional in that respect. I want to be more liberal in applying Jesus' teaching about "loving your enemies". I am having trouble loving the terrorists these days. I want to be more liberal in not rejecting folks who differ from me in their political beliefs or in their religious beliefs. After all, I remember a time when I was praying, several years ago, and God told me, "Donald, you should not be too critical of those who differ with you about spiritual beliefs because, actually, you are not totally correct either!"

So, I guess I really am a Fundamentalist, Conservative, Progressive, Liberal Baptist, and proud to be so. But actually, I believe that we would probably do well not to rely so much on labels where people are concerned. The old song said, "Red and yellow, black and white, they are precious in His sight." It doesn't sing as well but, "Fundamentalist, Conservative, Progressive, and Liberal, they are precious in His sight. Jesus loves the little children (and adults) of the world."

CHAPTER 21: SONGS OF OUR YOUNGER DAYS

Most of us will remember singing the songs and choruses of our younger days. Those of us who grew up during World War II will also remember the songs with a religious flavor that came out during those days. Would you remember these songs and sing them with me this morning?

DO LORD

I've got a home in Glory Land that outshines the sun. I've got a home in Glory Land that outshines the sun. I've got a home in Glory Land that outshines the sun, look away beyond the blue.

Do Lord, Oh do Lord, Oh do remember me. Do Lord, Oh do Lord, Oh do remember me,

Do Lord, Oh do Lord, Oh do remember me, way beyond the blue. Repeat.

JESUS LOVES THE LITTLE CHILDREN

Jesus loves the little children, all the children of the world, red and yellow, black and white, they are precious in His sight. Jesus loves the little children of the world. Repeat.

BATTLE HYMN OF THE REPUBLIC

Mine eyes have seen the Glory of the coming of the Lord, He is tramping out the vintage where the grapes of wrath are stored. He has loosed the fateful lightning of His terrible swift sword His truth is marching on.

Glory, Glory Hallelujah. Glory, Glory Hallelujah. Glory, Glory Hallelujah, His truth is marching on!

JACOB'S LADDER

We are climbing Jacob's ladder. We are climbing Jacob's ladder. We are climbing Jacob's ladder, soldiers of the cross.

Every round goes higher higher. Every round goes higher higher. Every round goes higher higher, soldiers of the cross.

Sinner do you love my Jesus? Sinner do you love my Jesus? Sinner do you love my Jesus? Soldiers of the cross.

DEEP AND WIDE

Deep and wide, deep and wide, there's a fountain flowing deep and wide.
Deep and wide, deep and wide, there's a fountain flowing deep and wide.

Wide and deep, wide and deep, there's a fountain flowing wide and deep.

Wide and deep, wide and deep, there's a fountain flowing wide and deep.

TURN YOUR EYES UPON JESUS

Turn your eyes upon Jesus, look full in His wonderful face, and the things of earth will look strangely dim, in the light of His glory and grace. Repeat.

OH, HOW I LOVE JESUS

There is a name I love to hear, I love to sing it's worth. It sounds like music in my ear the sweetest name of earth.

Oh, how I love Jesus. Oh, how I love Jesus, Oh, how I love Jesus, because He first loved me.

It tells me of a Savior's love who died to set me free. It tells me of His precious blood, the sinner's perfect plea.

Oh, how I love Jesus. Oh how I love Jesus, Oh, how I love Jesus, because He first loved me.

KUMBAYA MY LORD

Kumbaya my Lord, Kumbaya. Kumbaya my Lord, Kumbaya. Kumbaya my Lord Kumbaya, Oh Lord, Kumbaya.... Someone's singing. Someone's crying. Someone's praying.

OLD TIME RELIGION

Give me that old time religion, give me that old time religion, give me that old time religion,

It's good enough for me.

Makes me love everybody, makes me love everybody, makes me love everybody,

It's good enough for me. Repeat Chorus

It was good for Paul and Silas, it was good for Paul and Silas, it was good for Paul and Silas,

It's good enough for me. Repeat Chorus

IF YOU'RE HAPPY AND YOU KNOW IT

If you're happy and you know it clap your hands. If you're happy and you know it clap your hands,

If you're happy and you know it you can clap your hands and show it if you're happy and you know it, If you're happy and you know it clap your hands.

…......Say, "Amen"

…......Tap your toes.

THIS LITTLE LIGHT OF MINE

This little light of mine, I'm gonna let it shine, this little light of mine I'm gonna let it shine,

Let it shine, let it shine, let it shine.

…......Hide it under a bushel, no!...

…......Won't let Satan blow it out...

…......Let it shine 'til Jesus comes...

COMING IN ON A WING AND A PRAYER

Coming in on a wing and a prayer, coming in on a wing and a prayer,

Though there's one motor gone we will still carry on, we're coming in on a wing and a prayer!

PRAISE THE LORD AND PASS THE AMMUNITION

Praise the Lord and pass the ammunition, praise the Lord we ain't a goin' fishin',

Praise the Lord and pass the ammunition and we'll all stay free.

Oh, the sky pilot said it, you've got to give him credit, for a son-of-a-gun-of-a-gunner was he, Oh..

Praise the Lord and pass the ammunition, praise the Lord we ain't a goin' fishin',

Praise the Lord and pass the ammunition and we'll all stay free.

GOD BLESS AMERICA

God bless America, land that I love, stand beside her, and guide her,

Through the night with the light from above.

From the mountains to the prairies to the oceans white with foam,

God bless America, my home sweet home, God bless America, my home sweet home.

INTO MY HEART

Into my heart, into my heart, come into my heart, Lord Jesus. Come in today, come in to stay, come into my heart, Lord Jesus. Amen.

CHAPTER 22: OUR SPIRITUAL CONDITION

I wonder how you feel about where you are, spiritually? Do you have a set of spiritual standards that you measure yourself by and find your self "wanting"? Do you have a feeling, somewhere in the back of your mind, that you are somehow "letting God down" and that you ought to be more spiritual, or more like Jesus, somehow? Does that make you feel guilty sometimes?

Let me tell you how I think God feels about all of that. I don't have scripture and verse for this and to some extent it is just my speculation, based on my experience with God thus far. But I don't think I am too far wrong. First, I feel that, at our age, we are about as "spiritual" as we are likely to get during this life time. We might get a few more spiritual insights, but I doubt that we are going to change much more before God takes us back.

Secondly, God knows that and it's OK. God is not through with us yet and He will not be through with us when we leave this life. We are ETERNAL BEINGS just experiencing one phase of our eternal existence. We should not expect to learn everything we are suppose to learn in "the First Grade". We should expect gradual improvement, according to God's schedule, over a very long time. That does not mean that we should not be conscientious and that we should not keep trying to improve. But we need not "beat ourselves up" like we sometimes do. I honestly believe, that, when we graduate from our life on earth, that God will add what we have already learned and experienced to the spiritual maturity of our eternal soul.

I do not know what our next assignment might be but I do believe that when we breathe our last breath here we will just walk through a spiritual door into God's presence. We will continue to exist and continue to be aware, conscious, and that we will continue to be the same person. I believe that we will continue growing, learning, and having interaction with God and our friends and loved ones. It could be that we will come back to earth some day or go to some other type of place or existence that we can not even imagine right now. But I do not believe that we will simply cease to exist. Nor do I believe we will be in some sort of inactive state of sitting around Heaven for eternity or even just singing Hallelujah forever.

Thirdly, wherever we are right now in our spiritual development is O.K. I believe that God understands and accepts us and loves us just as we are now. That is what unconditional love is all about.

Fourthly, I believe that each of us WILL become more loving, more spiritual, more generous, and more mature as time goes on. It is really God accomplishing His work through us. And He has the rest of eternity to accomplish it.

So, let me encourage you to be joyful, knowing that, when you and I DO graduate from this present earth life, the very next word that we will hear will be God congratulating us for "a job well done". We will have nothing to be ashamed of, afraid of, or apologetic for. God will welcome us back to our home with as much love and excitement as any parent ever welcomed His son or daughter back after a long absence.

Prayer: Dear Father, I pray that I am correct in all of this. I can't know for sure as long as I am on this earth, but by faith I believe I am right. In Jesus name, Amen.

CHAPTER 23: THE RESUME

Suppose you were in a Personnel office and you had to hire someone for a very responsible job and a man came in to apply for the job and on his resume he had the following information: He had worked in 24 different jobs by the time he was 37 years old. You might conclude that he was not able to hold a job. What If those 24 jobs were in 14 different fields? You might conclude that he had difficulty making up his mind. What if, in these 24 jobs, 4 of them were as a grocery store worker, 4 were as a helper in a ship yard, 4 were as door to door salesman, and one was as a Temp worker? You might conclude that his work experience was all in menial type jobs, Right?

He doesn't sound too responsible, does he? What if, among those jobs he was a car washer and a gas station attendant and a Fuller Brush salesman and a Welcome Wagon visitor and a house painter and a grounds keeper? And now he hopes to get an IMPORTANT JOB? Well, don't be too quick to judge until you know the "Context" in which those jobs happened.

The first grocery store job was when he was 12

yrs. Old and just got his Social Security Card. The other three in the grocery store were on Saturdays when he was in High School. The helper jobs in the ship yard and the Fuller Brush job and a cook wear door to door sales job were when he was home for the summer during his college days. The house painting job, the Welcome Wagon door to door job, the gas station attendant job, and the job as a Temp worker were all after he was married and was a student in the Seminary. Oh, I didn't mention that his last 6 jobs were as Minister in five churches for 14 years and as a Chaplain for 21 years, retiring as the Chief Chaplain.

This is my resume that we are considering and I do not mean to be bragging so much as to say that facts can give the wrong impression when we do not know the whole story or when we do not know the context in which the facts take place.

The point is, every day we see people that we tend to judge on the basis of too few facts. For instance, here is a teen age girl with orange and purple hair. So, the color of her hair is orange and purple. What can we do with that? We might decide that she is lacking in self confidence and is just following every fad that comes along. Would you want her to baby sit your grand child? Not on your life.

But is the color of a teen ager's hair enough to tell

what is in her heart? Not at all. I know a teen age girl with purple hair who tells the children's story every Sunday morning at her church. And how about this, here is a lady whose language is unkind and whose attitude is almost 100% negative. You can hardly stand to be around her. It would be easy to judge her as choosing to be just a mean and cranky old woman. But we do not know all of the facts. We do not know that this woman has had a very hard time with her children and husband for years and that her body hurts all the time without relief. We just don't have enough facts to judge her.

Here is a man with a back pack on his back and he is unshaven. His clothes are ragged and dirty. He is probably homeless. We might look at him and decide that he is just lacking in ambition or he doesn't know how to manage his money. But we do not know enough about him to judge him. We missed the fact that he had to sell his home to buy expensive medicine for his dying wife. What I am saying is, that in almost any situation in which we try to judge another human being we are simply going to fail to be fair from the start, because we never know enough to judge. We don't know what it was like in his family. We don't know what she has been through in her life. And mostly, we don't know what God still has planned for that person.

God is not through with any of us yet.

I'm not saying that we have to like what they are like or what they are doing. I am just suggesting that, in every situation, we try to leave room for understanding, that we be willing to "give the benefit of the doubt", and that we remember that there is always more than "meets the eye". just remember that God would probably always be more pleased with us if we just leave ALL of the judging to Him. As I have said before, He always does more loving than judging anyway.

Of course, if you do happen to work in a personnel office, just try to be sure that you get all of the facts and not just a few.

Prayer: Dear Father. Help us to be patient, slow to anger, slow to judge and quick to love. In Jesus' name. Amen

CHAPTER 24: WHAT WAS "GOOD" ABOUT THE GOOD SAMARITAN?

Luke 10: 29 – 36. Read the Text.

This was an interesting conversation between one of the Religious Leaders and Jesus. The text says that the Leader was trying to trick Jesus. He was basically asking Jesus what he felt was necessary to please God with the way a person lives. Jesus turned the question around and asked the Leader what the Scriptures said. The man gave the classic answer: "Thou shalt love the Lord Thy God with all thy heart, and with all thy soul, and with all thy strength, and with all thy mind and thy neighbor as thy self. Jesus said that he had answered well. The man then continued to try to trip him up by asking "Well, just who is my neighbor?"

That is when Jesus told the story of the Samaritan. He did not really answer his question of "who is my neighbor". Instead, he told how a person should act toward his neighbor. So, what was really "Good" about the "Good Samaritan"?

Actually, Jesus never called him "good". That designation was added by tradition. But it was obvious that Jesus held up the actions of the Samaritan as an example of how a person should act toward other persons if he wants to please God. Let's just look at the basic actions that Jesus pointed out: Both the Priest and the Levite had seen the man lying wounded by the side of the road and chose to walk on the other side. It was probably assumed that they had done so because they would have become ceremonially unclean and unable to perform their religious duties if they had touched the wounded man.

The Samaritan, on the other hand, did the following things: He saw the man's condition and stopped anyway, because he felt compassion for the man. He committed himself to the man by giving him first aid from his own personal medicine, putting the man on his own personal transportation, causing the Samaritan to walk. He took the man to an Inn, knowing that it would cost him money. He spent the night caring for the man medically and then paid for special attention for the Inn Keeper to nurse the wounded man back to health. He guaranteed to pay the Inn Keeper for any additional expense that it might incur.

Now, what can we learn from the actions of the Samaritan that might help us to be pleasing to God with our everyday actions? First, that the feelings that we have are very important. The

Samaritan "felt" compassion. We do need to take our feelings seriously. We find that certain "feelings" are important to Jesus and thus to God. Compassion is one of those feelings. The feelings that are tied up in our relationship to God, loving Him with all of our heart, soul, strength, and mind. Those are feelings also. As we take inventory of our own feelings, if we find that we are lacking in compassion for the needs of other people and we are lacking in love for God, then that is something that should cause us some concern.

If we find that we don't really love our neighbors as ourselves, again we should take a moment to think about that. Lastly, the words about love DO say that we should love others as we love ourselves. So we should ask ourselves if we really DO love ourselves. Loving ourselves assumes that we love our bodies and that we take care of them as the Temple of the Holy Spirit of God. That, of course, means that we eat right and that we get enough exercise and enough rest. It also means that we do not do anything that we know is bad for our bodies, mind, or spirit.

If, after we consider all of this, if we find that there is room for improvement, then we should ask God to help us tend to that need of improvement. That is, if we really want to please our Heavenly Father.

As we ask ourselves about our compassion for our neighbors, we might ask ourselves how we can show that compassion in practical ways. The Samaritan "saw" the wounded man. Do we try to be as sensitive as possible to the needs and hurts that our friends and neighbors and, perhaps, even strangers are going through around us? Now I am preaching to the choir, because I know that you do take care of each other when some one has a personal loss or is sick or is obviously feeling bad. Let us continue to be like the "Good Samaritan" in our everyday life. In doing so we will be pleasing our Heavenly Father.

Dear Father: Please help us to have love and compassion for everyone who you allow us to come in contact with each and every day. In Jesus name. Amen.

CHAPTER 25: THE MANSIONS OF THE LORD

During the Memorial week I heard one of the most beautiful videos I have ever heard. I would encourage you to go to your computer and ask for "Video of The Mansions of the Lord". There are several versions and each one is worth seeing. It is made even more meaningful because it is usually sung slowly with scenes of soldiers in service being shown at the same time. It is sung, usually by a soldiers' chorus or college glee club. But it never fails to bring tears to my eyes. I am very happy to have Hepsi James with us again this morning to sing it for us. You have the words on the sheet that we passed out. As she sings I want you to imagine that you are not only hearing the song but you are viewing a group of soldiers carrying their brother to his final resting place in Arlington Cemetery in Washington. Imagine that you are seeing hundreds of simple white grave markers on the broad green lawn of Arlington.

THE MANSIONS OF THE LORD

To fallen soldiers let us sing
Where no rockets fly nor bullets wing
Our broken brothers let us bring
To the Mansions of the lord.

No more bleeding, no more fight
No prayers pleading through the night
Just divine embrace, Eternal light
In the Mansions of the Lord.

Where no mothers cry and no children weep
We will stand and guard though the angels sleep
All through the ages safely keep
The Mansions of the Lord. *

*The Mansions of the Lord, Written by J. Wilkes

I was so taken by the beauty of this hymn and the melody that I decided to try to put my own words to that tune – a song that would apply to you and me as the other applied to the soldiers. Here is what I have written to that tune and you have the words on your song sheet.

THE MANSIONS OF THE LORD   Additional
words by Don Hancock

To our loved ones who have gone before

And to those of us who approach that door

Let us have no fear as our spirits soar

To the Mansions of the Lord.

No more sickness no more pain

No more stress we're with God again

Just our Father's love to reign

In the Mansions of the Lord.

Where there is no sorrow, shame, or tear

Only the joy of eternal cheer

And we live forever with our loved ones dear

In the Mansions of the Lord.

Today happens to be Fathers' Day. Most of us
have lost our fathers And our mothers years ago.
But that word, "lost" I hope, has lost it's sadness
to you who have hope in seeing the Mansions of
the Lord. One of the great joys when we go to that

place, will be the seeing of all of our loved ones who have gone on before us to the Mansions that Christ promised to prepare for us.

If you ever find yourself doubting whether there WILL be Mansions of the Lord, or if we will see our loved ones some day in those mansions, let me remind you of the most encouraging phenomena in our modern times the "near death experiences, many of which you can hear online. While there can be a great deal of variation in the reports, there is enough similarity to support several conclusions. Heaven and its surroundings are beautiful beyond description and love is felt everywhere. God is not usually seen but He is strongly felt in that overwhelming love. One of the most recurring features is the presence of loved ones and friends that you have known before who come to you to welcome and comfort you. On this Fathers' Day let us be grateful to God for giving us loving mothers and fathers.

Prayer: Oh God accept our thanks to Thee

For giving life and liberty

And for our fathers who helped us see

The Mansions of the Lord. Amen

CHAPTER 26: WHY DO WE NEED GRATITUDE ANYWAY?

We are approaching Thanksgiving Day. If someone asked you, "out of the clear blue sky" what you are thankful for, you and I would probably have a pretty good answer - "I am grateful for my family, for my church, for life, for health." But beyond having that pat answer, how grateful are we, really? Let's look at gratitude for a few minutes together.

Why should we be thankful anyway? Is it really that important? Let's look at some reasons. First, there a seasonal reason. It is Thanksgiving season and so we all try to get into the "Thanksgiving Spirit" for a few days at least. Secondly, there is a cultural reason, because, all of our childhood our parents taught us to say,"Thank you". It is part of our training to be "good folks". People like a person who shows gratitude more than a person who is greedy, selfish, and ungrateful. Thirdly, there is a spiritual reason. Church and Sunday School, and the Bible has always taught us that God wants us to be grateful. Fourthly, there is a psychological reason. Getting ourselves into a state of gratitude takes us out of the stress created by greed and resentment and striving and "getting stuff" and puts us into a state of calmness and a sense of well being and feeling that "everything is going to be all right".

But, let's go back to the Spiritual reason for a moment. Being thankful because "God wants us to be Thankful". Sometimes we get the idea that God wants us to observe a bunch of "do's and don'ts – Ten Commandment sorts of things just because it is what He wants. Some times the Old Testament give us the idea that God has human shortcomings, like "God is Angry", "God is jealous", and we get the idea that perhaps God gives us these Commandments like "Be Thankful" just out of a need to "Lord it over us". But I don't think that is true at all. I believe that, when God tells us something that He wants us to do or NOT to do, it is for our benefit, not His.

In the case of Gratitude or Thankfulness, I believe that there are several Universal Spiritual Laws. "Love" is one of these laws. I believe that love has much more power than any of us has ever dreamed of. But Gratitude or Thankfulness is, I believe, another one of those Universal laws. I believe that every time we express real gratitude from our heart, either in word or deed or even feeling, that such an expression of gratitude does something to our spirit in an almost magical way. I believe that experience, however brief, opens up our spirits to God, opens up our experience of Heaven, in a sense, and brings us just a little closer to God.

So, how can we be more grateful? If I am not really feeling that sort of thankfulness already, how CAN I become that way? I am no expert, but I do have a few suggestions.

First, being Thankful is somewhat a matter of intention. Though there might be a few folks who seem to be just grateful by nature, most of us have to desire to become more grateful or it isn't likely to happen, with this one exception. In a few cases we become much more thankful after an illness or a near accident or almost losing a loved one. In that case we might become more grateful without having such a desire beforehand.

Secondly, as you have heard many times, it actually helps us to become more grateful if we periodically "count our blessings", become aware of how much we have in our lives to be grateful for.

Thirdly, it helps to say "Thank you every chance you get and mean it. Say it in response to kind acts – people holding a door for you, someone letting you in line in traffic, thank them with a hand wave. Seek out people to say "Thank you for service" - The Postman, Grocery Store Cashier, Soldiers, Policemen. There is something almost magical about saying Thank You. It actually seems to create more gratitude.

Fourthly, spend some time in the beauty of nature. Starry nights, singing birds, and beautiful fields of flowers seem to cause us to be grateful.

Lastly, ask God to help you be more grateful. God does not usually push Himself in uninvited. But if we invite Him to help us, He is glad to do it!

Let us pray: Dear Father. We DO want to be more grateful for all that you have given us. Please help us. In Jesus name. Amen.

CHAPTER 27: EMBRACING CHANGE

This morning I want to tell you about a very good friend and neighbor that my family has admired and loved for years. Her name is Dotsy. I am going to run a bit of a risk in that I want to share some things about her that have inspired and encouraged us over the years without at the same time invading her personal life or embarrassing her with too much praise, which she certainly deserves but would not feel comfortable if it is given too generously.

Change is one thing that happens in life and it happens to all ages. But when it happens to us in our latter years it can be more drastic, for our alternatives seem to dwindle as the years go by. When a young person loses the keys to his car, he gets another set of keys. When an older person "loses her keys" it means her driving days are over. Many changes have come into Dotsy's life while we have known her, but she has met them all with a spirit of wanting to do God's will. With that said, I must admit that she has sometimes met change with reluctance, aggravation, hesitation, and sometimes even "kicking and screaming", but always, finally, with a desire to please God.

I will mention just a few changes briefly. She lost her parents and then her four brothers over time. Each loss was, as it is to each of us, a unique and sad experience. She met each bereavement with love and patience and dependence on God. Those changes are common to all of us. But then Dotsy began to experience, one after the other, physical changes that would effect her life permanently. Both knees had to be replaced, then, without going into detail, she experienced at least three major chronic illnesses that she has had to have monitored by doctors. She did lose her ability to drive and now must trudge slowly with a walker on her constantly hurting legs to go anywhere that she goes. But she is thankful that she can still go places.

In spite of all this she still enjoys entertaining her friends with dinner and parties. In order to do this she must move around her kitchen from stove to sink to table by keeping one had on a sturdy object at all times. Yet she loves living in her home in spite of the difficulty in doing so.

But now she has finally reached the point when she can no longer live by herself. The threat to her safety is too great. She falls too easily. So far the falls have only resulted in bumps and scrapes but the next one might be more disastrous. So, for months the decision to move that she has been putting off has gotten closer and closer. This coming week is moving time.

She is moving to a Church Sponsored Retirement Community. She has been assigned a room and she knows how much she can take with her and how much she must "get rid of". Dotsy has been packing up her things and labeling them according to whether they will go with her, be sold, or be given away to her friends and loved ones.

All of this has been done reluctantly. She loves her home. She loves having friends over. She worries that things are going to be so different that she can no longer enjoy her life. Her friends have assured her that we will continue to visit her just as often as she can "stand us", but she wonders if that will be true or not. We assure her that the many activities at the home will keep her active. We truly believe this!

But perhaps the thing that gives her the most hope is that God will continue to let her serve Him as she has for her whole life. She has had a career as Head Librarian at Fort Gordon, the Army Base near Augusta, Ga., but she was basically letting God serve the soldiers through her. She has served in many capacities in her church, from historian to Librarian to leader in many of the church groups. She has enjoyed the fellowship of her fellow church members. But she is not able to do most of that any more.

What she does hope to do is to be used of God in her new surroundings to help her new friends in any way that her personality, talents, experience, and knowledge can be used by God to make their lives better.

Dotsy is a person who, though her body has had its struggles, is a vivacious personality with a razor sharp mind, who has very much to offer anyone who is privileged to meet her and get to know her. After having known her for 17 years, I believe that God has many ways that He plans to use her in the years before she goes back to be with Him in Heaven.

I might say the same thing about all of us who are either hearing or reading this devotional. Some of us, like Dotsy, will be going to Senior Living facilities of various types. Some might continue to live at home for a while and others will need to go live with their families as they become less independent. But ALL of us still have abilities, personalities, experience, and knowledge that God can use as we interact with the men, women, boys and girls with whom God allows us to have contact. And I honestly believe that God is eager to do just that, no matter what our age, infirmities, or handicaps might be. I hope that Dotsy's willingness will inspire you and me to be ready to do whatever God directs us to do. I believe God is willing and eager to use us until we take our final breath here and our next breath in His presence.

CHAPTER 28: TWO CONVERSATIONS

(This devotional was also included in two other devotional books, but I am including it here because it is probably my favorite and also because it has been so well received.)

One evening, as I was searching for a theme for this devotional, I noticed that "Fiddler on the Roof" was on the evening movie list. It is one of my favorite movies and I felt that, perhaps, God would use it to give me a subject. He did!

The movie is about Tevye, the village milk man, and his wife and daughters. The setting is Tsarist Russia in 1905. Tevye and his wife, Golde, were married in the traditional Jewish way, chosen for each other by a "match maker", with no thought of love or personal choice on the part of either.

Their lives were complicated because their three older daughters, within a short time, had made choices of husbands that defied their beloved tradition. The first daughter, after being promised to the local, well- to- do butcher, persuaded Tevye to give his permission for her to marry a poor tailor instead. Tevye did this, in spite of tradition, because he saw the "love in her eyes" for the tailor. This new experience of seeing love and marriage together caused Tevye to rethink his own marriage, and as he approached Golde a very beautiful musical conversation ensued.

Tevye: "Do you love me?"

Golde: "Do I what!?"

Tevye: "Do you love me?"

Golde: "Do I love you? For 25 years I've washed your clothes, cooked your meals, cleaned your house,given you children, milked your cow. After 25 years, why talk about love right now?"

Tevye: The first time I met you was on our wedding day. I was scared."

Golde: "I was shy."

Tevye: "I was nervous."

Golde: "So was I"

Tevye: "But my father and my mother said we'd learn to love each other, and now I am asking. Golde, do you love me?"

Golde: "I'm your wife!"

Tevye: "I know, but do you love me?"

Golde: "Do I love him? For 25 years I've lived with him, fought with him, starved with him. 25 years my bed is his, If that's not love, what is?"

Tevye: "Then you do love me."

Golde: "I suppose I do".

Tevye: "And I suppose I love you too."

Both: "It doesn't change a thing. But even so, after 25 years it's nice to know."

Now, as I heard this tender interchange, it dawned on me that this could be a conversation between God and myself. Let me present it to you just as I heard it.

God: "Donald, do you love me?"

Myself: "Do I what?"

God: "Do you love me?"

Myself: "Do I love you? I must be imagining this!"

God: "No, Donald. This is God and I am asking you a question. Do you love me?"

Myself: "Do I love You? For 69 years I've gone to church, Sunday School and Training Union. You remember Training Union, God?

God: "Yes, Donald. Was that 69 years ago? Yes, it was. I remember when we first met – really met. You were ten years old and you were at a funeral. It was the first time you realized that people really do die. For the first time you realized that some day you would be in a casket just like that."

Myself: "Yes, God. I was scared. Soon after that I became a Christian. The pastor said that I would learn to love you."

God: "So, do you love me?"

Myself: "For Heaven's sake, God. I'm a Christian!

God: "I know. But, do you love me?"

Myself: "Do I love Him? For 69 years I've prayed to Him, told other people all about Him, even built my career on Him, if that's not love what is?

God: "So, you DO love me?"

Myself: "God, if I know my heart, I love You more than anything else in the whole wide world!"

God: "And I love you too, Donald. More than anything else in the whole wide world! It doesn't change a thing but even so, after 69 years, it's nice to know."

God is still asking that question of each of us, and we each must answer as we see fit.

Let us pray. "Dear Father. We DO love you. Please help us to love you more. We ask in Christ's name. Amen"

CHAPTER 29: HOW DO YOU COMMUNICATE WITH GOD?

I want to ask you this morning, do you actually converse with God? For years I prayed in such a fashion that I would ask God a question and then hope for some vague feeling to come upon me, some sort of affirmation or feeling that would give me some sort of answer. Is that the way you pray now?

That is NOT the way it was in Bible times and that is not the way it HAS to be now. Moses had an actual CONVERSATION with God. God spoke to Moses and Moses spoke back to God. There are many other times when God, or His representative, an Angel, spoke to a human and the human spoke back. Mary the mother of Jesus had such a conversation and so did Peter and Paul and others.

You might think that such conversations happened only in the Bible but that is not true. I have discovered a way of prayer that is actually a conversation. I found that, if you expect an answer in your prayers that you will have it. I have given brief instructions on how to do this in other books and in fact I dedicated a whole book to giving a detailed 1,2,3 on how to do this. It is not difficult but, like other skills, it takes some practice. All it takes is simply enough faith in the process to just try it. I was skeptical when I heard about it, but I tried it about 12 years ago and it worked. I have used this method ever since.

I begin by praying that God would bless my praying with His presence and that I would not ask or say or do anything that would not be pleasing to Him. I always have a piece of paper and a pen, ready to write my part of the conversation and His part also. Then I usually ask if He has anything for me. I write it on the paper. If I have a question or a statement to begin, I write it down. Then I wait for an answer. I do not hear God's answer audibly. I am not "hearing voices" as such. I AM hearing very distinct thoughts that come as words just as surely as if I had actually heard them with my ears. This is usually the hardest part for beginners to do – to hear the distinct "thought words". Ordinarily a beginner will "hear" a thought and quickly say, "that could not be God speaking". If it is not distinct or if it does not seem to make any sense, it is simply that you are not used to praying in this way and it will take practice.

But I assure you that it does work, once you learn

how to do it. You might say that it is probably your own subconscious or even worse, the Devil. I can not prove that it is neither of these. All that I can say for sure is that the voice is always loving and Godly and helpful! That is a hard combination to consider being anything but from God. Many times I have needed help in such practical matters as getting a difficult nut to go on a bolt in a tight place that I had trouble getting to and I asked God for help and got it immediately. Yes, once you get used to hearing God speak, you can converse without writing it, but that takes a little bit longer. God gives me very specific answers and help in absolutely any problem that I have, from finances to how to put up a heavy picture on the wall. He also answers questions about what He wants me to do in particular right /wrong issues.

It is not really hard if you want to learn and if you will persevere. It usually does not happen with your first try, though I have a very good friend that actually was able to do it immediately and has done his praying that way ever since.

I hope that you will try it. If you are serious about it and you want more help, contact me at donh1654@comcast.net. I will send you more help. It is not something that you need to be afraid of. In the twelve years that I have used this method, I have never had a suggestion of anything negative, harmful, ungodly, or that you would call evil in any way.

CHAPTER 30: MOTHERS' DAY 1943

It was Mothers' Day, 1943, during World War II. 12 year old Bobby's mother was in bed with the flu. Bobby thought that she might feel better if he made her a hand made Mothers' Day Card and listed some of the good things she had done for him over the years and this is what he wrote:

"Dear Mama, I'm sorry that you are sick on Mothers' Day. I thought that it might make you feel better if I were to thank you for all the great things I can remember that you have done for me. I remember when I was little that you used to put me on your lap and tell me about Goldilocks and the three bears and about the mean old wolf that huffed and puffed and blew down the little pigs houses. I remember when I would have a bad dream and you would come in and help me know that I was all right.

I remember the time that the teacher caught me peeking at my spelling list during a spelling test and you had to come to school and talk to her and me together. I sure learned my lesson from that day. I never cheated a single time after that.

I remember when I played "Little Jack Horner" in the school play and you came to see me. I was so proud when everyone clapped and I saw you clapping the loudest! One year I wanted to go 'trick or treating' at Halloween and I didn't have a costume. You made me a home made 'Monster' costume.

I remember when I had a bad fever and you stayed up all night wiping the perspiration off of my face and taking my temperature. One Christmas I wanted a bicycle and there were no new bicycles to be had because of the war, but you bought me a nice used one that had been painted like new with your chicken and egg money.

I remember when I wanted to go to camp with the kids at church and you did without a new dress at Easter that I knew you wanted so that I could go to camp.

I remember when Daddy was going to use his belt on me for telling a fib and you talked him into just giving me a 'good talkin' to'.

The little boy named several other things and then said, "Thank you for being such a good Mama. Your son, Bobby." Then he took his "card" to his mother and she felt ever so much better after she read it. It wasn't very many days before she was back up and feeling great again.

Let's just imagine for a moment that your own son or daughter had made a similar list. Wouldn't it be great to have such a list? Most of our children would probably not think of sending us a list like that, but that does not mean that they are not grateful for all that you mothers have done for them.

Let's just take a few minutes to think of all the diapers that you washed, back when people actually washed diapers. Think of all the bed time stories you have read to them over the years and all of the times you were up at night feeding them and tending to them when they were sick. Think of all the times when you "took the neck of the chicken so that they could have the good parts".

Remember the times you worried about them just after they got their driver's license. Think of the times that you "did without" so that they could have something that they wanted. Think of the times you worried about them after they left home to go to school or to the military service or to their own marriage. Think of the times you have worried about them since then. And think of the many times you have worried about your grand kids.

Perhaps your children have already told you in

many ways how grateful they are for all that you have done and still do. I hope so. But if they haven't actually told you so in so many words, you can be pretty sure that in the private places of their heart, they really are grateful and , on this particular Mothers' Day, I would like to take it upon myself to speak for our children and even on behalf of God, to thank each and every one of you mothers for every one of the many, many times that you put your children ahead of your own comfort and desires and convenience. On behalf of everyone, let me say, "Thank you, Mom and Happy Mothers' Day.

Prayer: Thank You, God, for giving us our Mothers! Thank you for the memories of those that have gone ahead of us. Thank you for our children, who owe their lives and their welfare largely to the love and wisdom and sacrifice of their mothers. In Jesus name we thank you. Amen.

CHAPTER 31: LOVE MAKES THE WORLD GO ROUND

Sometimes I will get an idea for a devotional after I have already gone to bed and I will get up and write it down immediately. I have learned that, if I don't, the idea will be gone in the morning.

It happened the other night. Five minutes after I got in bed, I thought of a song: "Love Makes The World Go Round. I DID get up and write it down. The song was popular years ago. It went like this:

LOVE MAKES THE WORLD GO ROUND

LOVE MAKES THE WORLD GO ROUND,

YOUR PULSE WILL BEAT AND YOUR HEART WILL POUND

CAUSE LOVE MAKES THE WORLD GO ROUND.

Sometimes we think of love as just another good thing, like kindness, faithfulness, gratitude, faith , hope, or good works. All of these things are good and are needed, but I believe that when we lump Love in with all of the rest, we miss something very important. Love is somehow different from the rest.

Paul realized that to some extent in I Cor. 13 when he said, "Faith, hope, love, these three, but the greatest of these is Love. But even Paul might have missed something. I think that Love is even more than just "the greatest of these". I believe that Love is in a whole different category from all the rest. That is why we say "God is Love". God doesn't just HAVE love. He IS Love. If that is the case, then the VERY ESSENCE of God is Love. In 1 John 4:8 it says, "He that loveth not knoweth not God, for God IS love." I don't think the Bible ever said "God is Faith" or "God is Hope" or God is Good Works. What the Bible is saying is that, the very ESSENCE of God is love. To NOT know love is to NOT know God.

There are places in the Bible that say or insinuate that Love Was what motivated God in the first place. It is hard for us to wrap our minds around what it was like in the very beginning, before creation. But as far as we have been told, there was just the triune God – Father, Son, and Holy Spirit. But then there was something that moved them to create the universe, the world, and mankind. That something was not any of those wonderful things like faith or hope or kindness or gratitude, as good as they are. It was love. If that is the case, it makes love pretty special doesn't it? Not only does "Love make the world go round" but maybe Love made the world in the first place. Maybe, in some way that we do not understand, Love keeps everything going.

The Bible said that God gave Solomon great wisdom. But, if Solomon had REALY been wise he would have followed up by asking God to give him Love.

What do you ask God for? Anything? If you DO ask God for anything in particular, what sort of things do you ask for? Enough income to keep going day by day? That's a good request. Reasonably good health? That is a good request, especially if you are sick or hurting. Do you ask to know and do His will? Now you are getting to where God wants you to be. But if you really want to ask God for the very best that He has to offer, ask Him to let you be filled with LOVE, to be motivated by LOVE, to be guided by LOVE, strengthened by LOVE, comforted by LOVE, disciplined by LOVE, fed by LOVE, satisfied by Love, and, in the end, welcomed home by LOVE. If you ask that, you are simply asking to be like Jesus. That is not TOO MUCH TO ASK.

Dear Father. Help us not to want anything in this world as much as we simply want to have LOVE like Jesus did. In His name, Amen.

CHAPTER 32: A BEAUTIFUL SONG

Several nights ago my wife showed me what looked like a poem of some sort. It was titled "Blessings" by Laura Story. It looked familiar but I could not "place it". I read the words and it dawned on me that it was a song that I had heard somewhere and that the words really had a powerful message. "Let me see if I can find a video of the song on the computer so that you can hear it." We listened to it and I was very touched but I still could not remember where I had heard it. I was thinking to myself, "I bet Lee Menefee would love this song, I will give her a copy (Lee Menefee is a friend who sings in the choir and often sings solos). At the very moment that I was thinking that, my wife remembered where she had heard it. She said, "This is the song that Lee Menefee sang as a special last Sunday!" It's funny how the mind works, isn't it?

Well, I don't think that Laura Story would mind me sharing her song with you this morning, so that all of us can receive the full benefit of her thoughts, even if you heard it sung last Sunday.

BLESSINGS

We pray for blessings
We pray for peace
Comfort for family, protection while we sleep
We pray for healing, for prosperity
We pray for Your mighty hand to ease our
suffering
All the while, You hear each spoken need
Yet love us way too much to give us lesser things

'Cause what if Your blessings come through
raindrops
What if Your healing comes through tears
What if a thousand sleepless nights
Are what it takes to know You're near
What if trials of this life are Your mercies in
disguise

We pray for wisdom
Your voice to hear
And we cry in anger when we cannot feel You
near
We doubt Your goodness, we doubt Your love
As if every promise from Your Word is not
enough
All the while, You hear each desperate plea
And long that we have faith to believe

'Cause what if Your blessings come through
raindrops

What if Your healing comes through tears
What if a thousand sleepless nights
Are what it takes to know You're near
And what if trials of this life are Your mercies in
disguise

When friends betray us
When darkness seems to win
We know that pain reminds this heart
That this is not, this is not our home
It's not our home

'Cause what if Your blessings come through
raindrops
What if Your healing comes through tears
And what if a thousand sleepless nights
Are what it takes to know You're near
What if my greatest disappointments
Or the achings of this life
Is the revealing of a greater thirst this world can't
satisfy
And what if trials of this life
The rain, the storms, the hardest nights
Are Your mercies in disguise

This song is so powerful, so wise. It contrasts how
we pray for "good things", for "easy things" for
"comforting things" like peace and protection and

prosperity, while, all the time God knows that what we might really need in order to grow and mature is some hard times, some tears and some "rain on our parade.

I hope that these devotionals have helped you to stay close to God.

CHAPTER 33: LET'S NOT TAKE CHRISTMAS FOR GRANTED

Most of us assume that we can celebrate Christmas every year in any way that we wish. We will probably celebrate it this year with all the trimmings. But that is nsot true for everyone. There are countries where Christians are persecuted and must worship and celebrate Christmas, Easter and other Christian holidays quietly behind closed doors with fear and trembling.

But there are situations, even in our own country when Christmas celebrating must be done in secret. I recently heard of such a situation. My wife and I were visiting a member of our church. She had a large, glass case full of beautiful dolls. I asked her how she happened to get started collecting dolls. She said, "There IS a story behind that!"

Then she told us the story. "When I was a little girl of six years old, with a sister that was seven, we had a father who belonged to a church that did not believe in celebrating Christmas. They believed in the Bible but not in Christmas celebrations. My father was a very strict member of his church. In fact, the group met in our house every week. My mother was 15 years younger than my father and was somewhat dominated by him."

"She had grown up in an evangelical church and had always enjoyed church before she married my father. When Christmas came, my mother wanted my sister and I to enjoy Christmas as much as possible. We lived out in the country and had a small forest of trees in the back of our house. My mother cut strips of colored paper and we went out into the edge of the forest and found a tree that looked like a Christmas tree. She hung the strips of paper on the tree and did her best to make it 'Christmasy'."

"On Christmas eve she would "smuggle" a doll out to the tree for us to find on Christmas day. It was usually one doll for the two of us. We would leave the doll out by the tree and go out there to play with it. We dared not bring it home. One year our older brother gave us one bicycle between us. When my father asked if it was a Christmas present he had to lie and say, 'No, it is just that they are at an age when they need to have a bike.' If he had admitted that it was a Christmas present, my father would probably have made him take it back."

"When I grew up and had my own home, I would get the tallest Christmas tree I could find for my living room, and I would get any doll and as many dolls as I wanted. That is how my collection of dolls began."

I asked her, "Do you have any of those original dolls in your collection?"

"No," she said, "Sadly, each doll had to be left out at the tree all the time. After a year of wind and rain, each doll would be ruined."

Well, it is stories like that which should remind us that Christmas is much more to be cherished as not just a business sales opportunity or a chance to have a holiday. It should be a cherished time for two reasons. Because it is when we celebrate the birth of Jesus AND because many people around the world today and also many people down through the ages have not been able to celebrate Christmas freely and without the fear of consequences. Let us be careful that we never allow ourselves to take Christmas time for granted. Let us pray. Dear Father, Thank You for the gift of your Son and for the time of Remembrance that we call Christmas.

I hope that these devotionals have helped you to stay close to God.

THE END FOR NOW

Donald C. Hancock   Augusta, Ga.

October, 2016

donh1654@comcast.net